Understanding the

ANGELS

Dr. James Hodges

ECKO Publishing, P. O. Box 901930, Sandy, UT 84092

Word Ministries products are available at special quantity for bulk purchase for bookstores, churches, fundraising and sales promotion. For information, send request to: Word Ministries, P. O. Box 928, Livonia, LA 70755. Email contact may be sent to jameshodges@lightandlamp.com

Understanding the Angels by Dr. James Hodges
Published by ECKO Publishing
P. O. Box 901930
Sandy, UT 84092
www.lightandlamp.com

Unless otherwise indicated, all Scripture quotations are taken from the King James Version of the Bible.

Scripture quotations marked AMP are from the Amplified Bible. Old Testament copyright © 1965, 1987 by Zondervan Corporation. The Amplified New Testament copyright © 1954, 1958, 1987 by the Lockman Foundation.

Scripture quotation marked TLB are from The Living Bible. Copyright © 1971. Used by permission of Tyndale House Publishers, Inc., Wheaton, IL 60189. All rights reserved.

Cover design by my daughter, Kelly Sanders

Library of Congress Control Number: 2009940940
ISBN: 978-1-61658-303-3

Dedication

To my dad who is deceased, yet he taught me the importance of the study of the Word of God.

To my loving wife, Karen, your encouragement and inspiration are the greatest assets in my life. I will always be in debt to you for the happiness which you have brought me.

Acknowledgments

I could not have completed this project, had it not been for my great wife. Her love and internal drive for those things of the kingdom – all have given me the greatest inspiration to see that this series is completed and given to help others. For the many days and nights in which I lived in another world while writing the manuscript and to the final publication. Especially for those endless hours in which she would continually read the manuscript searching for errors.

My personal and great friend – Bishop George Austin – your energies and encouragement have been such an inspiration. Your insatiable love for the work of the Lord and your drive to see that all of mankind has the opportunity to feel the true presence of God in their life; you have been most encouraging.

Table of Contents

Preface

Consequently, they had never met. His world existed in an earthly canal enclosed by a curtain which hung from stainless steel rods attached to the ceiling. On the other side of the door anxiously awaited his first contact in life. He had no idea of the compassion that lived in the stranger's eyes, the warmth of their hands; in fact, the physical structure was of no importance at all. They had never passed in the night nor spoken on the telephone.

Within a few moments the stranger entered the room wearing a clean pressed white robe, a surgical mask to cover the nose and eyes along with the tan-shaded gloves which would be used. The procedure was very familiar to him; it had been performed thousands of times before over the years. Although each one brought a special feeling of accomplishment, it was a natural procedure.

In a short period of time, a newborn child would pass through the birth canal and enter into the world. These glove protected hands that would hold the innocent up and with a swift slap on its tiny cheeks – air would pass into the lungs which God had given it. Life would begin to work on its own; no longer needing the mother to give all she had.

As family and friends would gather into the small room, the attention would shift from a mother who was expecting the child which had been born. Each would hold the infant and marvel at this added dimension of life. The talk would focus on whose features were carried in the physical structure; the eyes, hairlines, ears and the bulkiness of the nose. But, along with all the talk and excitement – one sound could not and would not be heard.

Neither the mother, father, visiting friends or family members were given the responsibility for reminding the newborn babe how to breathe. No one would have ever imagined of whispering the vital instructions of keeping life to this child. In fact, not one concerned friend or family member was ever inclined to remind this bundle of joy that if he did not keep breathing he would die. Also, during the delivery by the doctor, there was no set of instructions to tell the baby when to smile or frown, let him know that if he cries it is a sign that he is hungry or wet or when he can throw that "cute" little fit when he is upset or hurting. All of these reactions, which are natural, automatically come to each of us at birth.

The actions now were important, but not the most. Avenues would be walked, streets would be viewed from afar and up-close, each reaction of the eyes would reflect the human response to how this newborn child would view life and live the rest of his or her life. The society in which they were raised would directly determine the outcome that many would judge years and even decades from now.

The manner in which this innocent child would be taught about the natural and supernatural world would have significant influence on his development. Whether or not he would live a successful life, live in poverty, show compassion or reflect unhappiness is now all in the hands of the "teachers" to whom he had been given by God. Although life in the natural is important, the supernatural or spiritual side provides the most promising and guaranteed happiness; it is the only one that really counts since it will last forever.

Introduction

"I write unto you, fathers, because you have known him that is from the beginning. I write unto you, young men, because you have overcome the wicked one. I write unto you, little children, because ye have known the Father."

I John 2:13

Introduction

Walking in the Spirit, having communion with God should be a natural environment to the born again believer. We have made this avenue of spiritual warfare seem mystical, almost unattainable; giving it a "hocus pocus" view and that for those who are "way out there." It is not the intentions of this author to, for one moment, take away the awesomeness and beauty of a move of God. As we examine the scriptures, let each of us realize that this walk should be just as natural.

Allow me for this one moment to react to a situation which I just experienced. A number of weeks before this book was scheduled to be written, I was at a retreat with business men on the top of a mountain in North Carolina. As these men began to pray, found areas of God which brought depth, satisfaction and greater hunger; each seems to ask the same question. *How are these levels attained and how can I get there?* Many expressed the desire for such a fulfillment in their life, although their friends and sometimes Pastors spoke against it.

I look back to the man of God who dedicated me, a prophet and one who daily walks in this supernatural realm. The late Reverend T. W. Barnes did not labor to get there, did not write himself notes as a reminder; but lived it every moment of each day. It is just as natural as breathing. It is for this cause he can walk into a room and take control over the spirits of death and sickness, evil spirits and thoughts which haunt many men and women. Constantly in touch with the Courts of Heaven, his life is an example of what is meant in the writings of scripture pertaining to the new birth and being born again (St. John 3:1-7).

As I look at the book of Zechariah, beginning with chapter 1; we can see the invisible agents and forces of God. Verse 9 gives us insight to a conversation between the writer and Jehovah which began in the first verse; ". . . And the angel that talked with me said unto me, I will shew thee what these be." (vs. 9) As we go through the word of God and search the scriptures, here we can find those benefits that come from a born again lifestyle. Yes, being born again (living like a true Christian) is a lifestyle. There is more than just a Sunday morning and midweek service to "living in the Spirit."

We have been raised in a society which advocates the attitude of "just getting by" and this philosophy has been taken up by Christianity. We can barely afford to live, and a sad case to be made is neither can we afford to die. A matter of survival – making ends meet, just making it, somewhere it will get better; all these have entered into the minds and hearts of the religious. The world never was meant to have this type of affect on the church, just the opposite is true.

Why live in defeat; barely exist when the forces of Heaven are at our disposal? The only real world is the spirit world. Look around you, everything you see is temporal according to II Peter 3:10 and will be destroyed. To truly live (and not merely exist), one must become involved completely in the spiritual world. As we understand the power which has been made accessible through the Holy Spirit, and being assured of the covenant of the New Testament; then victory which can be attained with the renewed mind will take us to victory. We do not need to run any longer, it is time to stand up and use the power within you by the Spirit of God. Spiritual graduation is available to all – this is the desire of the Father.

When the thought of an angel is mentioned, an individual will think of Guardian Angel which is most often talked about, others will think of the Archangels, Cherubims or the Seraphims. We fail to realize how many classifications and types there are to the mighty army of heaven. There are seven different types of ministering angels -- simply waiting for us to request their services.

Many of our spiritual issues have never been settled because of the lack of knowledge which we possess. We can live a life of greater awareness and a lot less frustration when understanding the potential which each individual has at their disposal. These heavenly warriors stand to not only protect us, but to battle in our behalf. The reason most live such a deprived lifestyle is because they know of no other way to live. When we understand the organizational structure and the use of these "beautiful creatures" in our life -- success and happiness will be ours.

It is needful for us to realize that the angels of God ascend and descend from heaven to earth daily, as shown in the vision to Jacob in the book of Genesis. If every individual could realize that with every struggle we have, we are not alone; but there is at least one angel standing with us to defend us from all our enemies.

There are over one hundred million angels. They are likened to the numbering of the stars of the heavens. Each has their place and desire for you to use them. Angels have been on earth and visited men like Abraham, Moses, Joshua, David, Zechariah, the Virgin Mary, Jesus, Peter, Paul, John and others. Whether they are seen or not, these angels are available to assist the believer whenever they are needed and are directed by God. There are two of God's angels to every fallen angel; and God's angels are on our side.

In the book of Genesis, chapter three, only one devil is mentioned and called the old serpent. With over fifty million demons that exist were not made known to us in this book. This is one third of the total angels of God. Revelation, chapter five, reveals that there are ten thousand times ten thousand plus thousands of thousands of God's angels. Therefore, the fallen angels numbering one out of three; this would make for over one hundred fifty million original angels of God.

No one can actually say how many angels there are, the number is innumerable. Hebrews 12:22 says, "But ye are come unto mount Sion, and unto the city of the living God, the heavenly Jerusalem, and to an innumerable company of angels." In II Kings 6:16; during a siege from the enemy, the prophet Elisha prayed for God to reveal to the servant that the forces of heaven were with them. After the prayer, the servant looked into the heavens and saw the company of angels which Jehovah had sent for their protection. The reply found in this scripture, "And he answered, Fear not: for they that be with us are more than they that be with them."

Job gives us the perfect answer when referring to the numbering of the angelic hosts of heaven. "Is there any number of his armies? and upon whom doth not his light arise?" (Job 25:3) There is no sure way of knowing accurately how many there are, but one thing stands to be true – we know they are there and have been sent by God to help mankind.

From The Beginning

One of the most fascinating things about humanity is the ability to acquire traits, features and expressions which are found in their offspring. It is amazing how a child can be born and within a few days begin to show traits which exist in the parents, without ever having been taught a single one. Facial expressions, hand movements, attitudes and demeanor will quickly manifest themselves in children.

Genesis 1:27 says, "So God created man in his own image, in the image of God created he him; male and female created he them." When God blew the breath of life into man, there were certain "traits" which man acquired from his heavenly father (Gen. 2:7). As we look closer, we can find our example in the life of Jesus Christ.

As we look at the scriptures, we know that Mary was the tool of which God would use to bring Jesus Christ into the world (Matthew 1:23). In Matthew 1:20, the angel of the Lord appeared unto Joseph and said, ". . .for that which is conceived in her is of the Holy Ghost." Jesus would have the attributes of his father, God. Let us examine the traits which Jesus had.

A troubled heart – John 14:1
The heart of God – John 1:18
A comforting heart – John 14:18
A loving heart – John 15:9
An honest heart – John 16:7
A witnessing heart – John 15:27
A compassionate heart – John 16:29-33
A submissive heart – John 17:1
A burdened heart – Luke 22:42
An interceding heart – John 17:9
A burning heart – John 17:20-26

Modern Society

The desire of greatness is all too familiar in our society. The supernatural expressions which have made themselves present in this society did not start in the last few years. One of the leading factors in the fall of man was a statement made by the serpent in the Garden of Eden to Eve. Although the statements made by the serpent were untrue, when the conversation hinted at a challenge to their greatness, "then your eyes shall be opened, and ye shall be as gods," (Gen. 3:5) – Eve was more than ready to respond. One translation from the book of Ecclesiastes chapter three, verse eleven says, ". . also he hath set eternity in the heart of man . ."(NASB). The desire of the heavenly nature was given to man from his very beginning.

Man's quest for the supernatural has transcended time in plays, comic books and modern television. In 1976, we saw the debut of the comic action heroes with *Mego*; only to be followed by *Super Knights, Super Pirates, Robin Hood* and many more. Television shows such as *Bionic Man, Wonder Woman, Batman and Robin* have fueled the minds of the young and old as to the search for supernatural relationships. Later, Hollywood began producing and promoting shows such as *Touched by an Angel, Highway to Heaven*, *Michael*, and *City of Angels* in the reach for that inner desire which man was seeking to fulfill.

(Please allow me to pause at this point and validate the study and personal experiences with God's Mighty Army of Angelic hosts. I have experienced encounters with all types of angels – both good and bad. The greatest asset man has within his reach are the forces of heaven which stand at attention to be called upon.)

In 1994, the American Booksellers Association stated that it was the year for angels and angel related books. This subject was the most popular category on the exhibit floor and a number of New York publishers released titles on angels – many from a New Age perspective. A total of thirty-two books were scheduled for release in February 1995. Many books have been written on angels, but only a handful of them have provided an actual view from the Bible.

Once again, we will explore the use of angels as taught in the Bible. Many have stayed away from the detailed study of these "fighters of God" because of the lack of experience and the fear of having them misrepresented. When we understand their place in respect to ours, it is easy to view them as "agents" of God who are meant to aid our walk and give us continual victory in our life. They are not meant to give us "any thing" we want nor to serve us as a "getting even" agent; they are to be used in reference to the Kingdom of God on our behalf.

The Initial Encounter

I was raised in an average town in a small church. Just like many Christians today, I was told about a life of fulfillment and joy, victorious living – only never told all the ways to have them. The "concept" of this lifestyle had troubled me since the age of nine. As I began to seek for the answers, a feeling of accomplishment did not come until fourteen years later. When studying the scriptures one evening – the revelation of all which I was not told came while reading my Bible for a Sunday morning lesson.

In the fall of 1980, a member of the congregation was in the intensive care unit for an apparent heart attack. While standing there, my eyes and spirit were drawn to a man who stood hopelessly alone in the corner. I approached him and asked why his demeanor was so down cast and his appearance was one of rejection. He informed me that his son was given only a few days to live. My spirit jumped from within me and without ever thinking about the words, I asked if I could pray for him.

Grabbing me by the hand, the troubled father led me to the window – only to see his son from the distance. I asked the nurse if I could anoint him with oil and pray for him. It was from her that I was informed that he also had a contagious disease. I placed my hands against the glass and asked the angels of healing to go where I could not and do the work which I could not perform. I turned and asked the father if he would believe – his response actually caught me off guard; "I believe it has been answered."

Late that night the phone rang with the sound of a screaming gentleman on the other end of the line. "My son has set up in bed and asked for food!" Three days later, the son went home and returned back to work.

Meeting Evil Forces

In the summer of 1981, I had finished a fast and gotten up early one morning for a time of prayer. I was somewhat weary from the fasting but knew I must have the time of prayer and devotion for the events of the day. While I was washing my face for a feeling of freshness, a voice began to speak to me. "Why don't you just take your life?" "Nobody cares a thing about you."

The sound of the voice and its sense of persuasion were very chilling. Before I knew what I was doing, I spoke back and told the unwanted visitor to be quiet and commanded him to leave. The discourse lasted only for a matter of minutes but it seemed like an eternity.

A number of hours had passed and I had almost forgotten about the incident when a lady in my church came running up to me – exhausted and out of breath; she related an event which happened to her before the sun had risen. She was trembling from the fear which had compassed her from what the angel had told her when she was awakened.

The following is the story she related to me: “Early this morning I felt a hand shake me from my sleep to get me out of bed to pray. The angel told me to get up and pray for you, since your life was in danger. She was told by the angel to intercede for me, it was the only hope I had of survival.” Her last remarks were, “I am so glad to know you are still alive.”

There have been a number of events in my life of angelic visitations. As we continue in this book, I will explain them and give you the basics for a life of victory and hope. Read and study with an open mind, let the Spirit of the Lord guide you.

"But I beseech you, that I may not be bold when I am present with that confidence, wherewith I think to be bold against some, which think of us as if we walked according to the flesh.

For though we walk in the flesh, we do not war after flesh:

(For the weapons of our warfare are not carnal, but mighty through God to the pulling down of strong holds;)

II Corinthians 10:2-4

The Angels

"Bless the Lord, ye his angels, that excel in strength, that do his commandments, hearkening unto the voice of his word."

Psalms 103:20

Chapter One

The Angels

The Bible clearly advocates the existence of angels. These ambassadors of God, members of the Court of Heaven, and servants of the Most High stand at attention to do that for which each was created. These ministering spirits (Psalms 104:4) are much more than a figment of our imagination, and even though they are not taught about much – they are to aid each believer in their successful walk through this journey called life. As we examine these beautiful "creatures" in the chapters ahead; take note at the various orders of power and authority given to them. Of the seven different classifications, let us from the examples of the scriptures and personal experiences in life; learn how the word defeat will become one of the past.

It is imperative that we live successfully in the Will of God, as earthly ambassadors – we also have access to the Court of Heaven. Let me add, this does not promote "angel worship" and is not intended to do so. God is the only Supreme One and even though the angels are of "innumerable number" (Hebrews 12:22), they alone cannot bring salvation. God uses men, they are the tool through which He moves and each of us can use the source of power given from the King of Kings.

When a born again believer understands the power and authority through the Name of Jesus; then the ministering spirits can be properly used. This "family" benefit comes as the Name and the blood are applied to all. Each must leave the carnal mind behind and look with the vision of faith which naturally cannot be seen. Since the senses of man (sight, hearing, touch, taste and smell) are nothing but a distraction to the spiritual man; it is essential that we see through eyes of faith, only that which is revealed by the Spirit of God from the Word.

As we enjoy their ministry, another arsenal has been placed in our hands. Why should we leave weapons sitting on the shelf when the adversary will use all he has against us? The whole purpose of Jesus Christ was to bring victory to each and every human that would ever live and just as He had access to the Heavenly Court --- by the adoption we do also.

It will be mentioned often, not as a reminder; but to emphasize the importance of prayer in a successful spirit filled life. For each man or woman to reach out into the superior realm of God's ministering angels – it will take a desire which comes only with an obsession. Nothing can deter you! Though they may exist (with natural vision), there are no walls, boundaries or circumstances which will hinder me! I can only see through eyes of faith, only that which is revealed by the Spirit of God.

Understanding Purpose

Just as local, state and federal governments exist, so also does the spirit world. There is a chain of command, those who are assigned certain duties or tasks to perform. In understanding their responsibilities, it is easier for us to take advantage of the different parts played by each order and rank. When meetings are held in the natural order of government, *Roberts Rules of Order* is often obeyed since they give regulation to what could be a confusing and frustrating situation. As in the natural setting, the same can be said about the spirit world.

The earth is only the visiting place for the angels; their primary place of existence is at the throne room with God. This is seen clearly from the vision of the angels ascending and descending in the book of Genesis – a vision which Jacob had. They are given their "marching orders" from God and go about to do the work which has been assigned to them. Matthew 22:30 and John 1:51 will bear out the fact of their dwelling place.

There are often misconceptions when understanding what "heaven" is like or the location of it. When the bible speaks of the heavens; there are actually three locations which are being mentioned. The first heaven is the atmosphere or the clouds which we see above us. The second heaven is the stars and planetary regions which we are required to see with the naked eye and the use of a telescope. The third heaven is the realm where God abodes with the angels in his kingdom. This area cannot be seen with the naked eye or the telescope. It is believed this is the heaven which John the Revelator saw in a vision "coming down from God out of heaven" in the book of Revelation. This thought is also mentioned in Jude 6, where Jude wrote about a special dwelling place. Jude 6 says, "kept not their first estate, but left their own habitation."

When Satan was cast out of Heaven because of his pride and rebellion, a large group of the angels came with him and the same "government" type system was set up on the earth. Why would it not seem proper that the angels whether from Heaven or thrown from Heaven would possess the same type of power and control. Those created to give service to God and do the work of God on the earth at the same time can bring havoc when they have been cast out of the heavens and sentenced to the "chains of darkness."

> Isaiah 14:12 says, "How art thou fallen from heaven, O Lucifer, son of the morning! how art thou cut down to the ground, which didst weaken the nations!"

> Ephesians 6:12 says, "For we wrestle not against flesh and blood, but against principalities, against powers, against the rulers of the darkness of this world, against spiritual wickedness in high places."

In looking at the scriptures, there are some distinctive implications that the intelligence forces of heaven (which God controls) is caring on His government are indeed the angels. The name does not denote their nature as we would know it, but their position or office as messengers of God. From the early beginning with Abraham and throughout the scriptures we find these "forces" at work for the kingdom of God.

Genesis 18:2, 22 – Abraham at Mamre

Joshua 5:13, 15 - Joshua at Gilgal

Genesis 32:24, 30 – Jacob at Peniel

Spiritual Beings

The angels are heavenly hosts, ambassadors to the throne, created beings by and for God. These spiritual beings or ministering spirits have been known to appear in visible forms, yet they are spirits. They are neither male nor female for sex and gender are not issues with these ministering spirits. A number of scriptures give reference to our understanding of these special representatives of the Lord. Luke 20:35-36 says, ". . . neither marry, nor are given in marriage: Neither can they die any more: for they are equal unto the angels;" Let us also examine other scriptures which tell us that they are spiritual beings and cannot have offspring.

> Notice the phrase in Mark 12:24, "Do ye not therefore err, because ye know not the scriptures, neither the power of God?" along with Matt 22:30, "For in the resurrection they neither marry, nor are given in marriage, but are as the angels of God in heaven."

As often seen in the artist rendition, angels do not have wings and a "halo" over their heads. As we look at the different types of angels, Seraphim and Cherubim are pictured with as many as six wings. They may differ to their duties and responsibilities to God and to serve mankind, but the fact remains they are holy and sinless. Also consider that there are some who “fell” at the time of Lucifer, this has given consideration to the fact that they have some “free will” in their destiny.

There is no such thing as death for the angels. Not only are they sexless (neither male nor female), but being from the beginning and created by God; they cannot die. Those who left the splendor of Heaven, the majesty of the throne with the fall of Lucifer when he rebelled, are still alive and will remain so until their judgment. (Let it be noted even though this study has not been determined to cover such; but the scripture tells us that Hell was originally created for Satan and his angels.) For the sake of knowing the difference, a separate chapter will be written for knowledge and understanding of these particular angles.

We are told in II Peter 2:4, “For if God spared not the angels that sinned, but cast them down to hell, and delivered them into chains of darkness, to be reserved unto judgment;” We are also told in Jude 6, “And the angels which kept not their first estate, but left their own habitation, he hath reserved in everlasting chains under darkness unto the judgment of the great day.”

When we are born again of the water and the spirit, we are raised above them and can enjoy the benefits of their ministry. When God created man (Genesis 1:27), he was given dominion on the earth. Even though mankind is of the earth, and the angels are heavenly hosts; we as Children of God can access the throne with the wealth of Heaven and its powers. When we live and walk in the Spirit; as heirs of salvation and carry the Name of Jesus, the authority goes with us.

Hebrews 1:14 says "Are they not all ministering spirits, sent forth to minister for them who shall be heirs of salvation?"

Psalms 104:4 says "Who maketh his angels spirits; his ministers a flaming fire:"

The existence and order of angelic beings can only be understood and discovered from the Scriptures. While the Bible does not treat this particular subject specifically, there are quite a number of incidents which show in detail the existence of these "beings." Let us take notice of a few of these scriptures:

> Genesis 16:7; "And the angel of the Lord found her by a fountain of water in the wilderness, by the fountain in the way to Shur."
>
> Genesis 16:10; "And the angel of the Lord said unto her, I will multiply thy seed exceedingly, that it shall not be numbered for multitude."
>
> Genesis 16:11; " And the angel of the Lord said unto her, Behold, thou art with child, and shalt

bear a son, and shalt call his name Ishmael; because the Lord hath heard thy affliction."

Matthew 28:2; "And, behold, there was a great earthquake: for the angel of the Lord descended from heaven, and came and rolled back the stone from the door, and sat upon it."

Hebrews 1:4; "Being made so much better than the angels, as he hath by inheritance obtained a more excellent name than they."

Order and Power

Not all angels have the same power and authority, but according to their power and duties there seems to be various ranks and orders among them. Even though they may not all have the same rank or power, this does not in any way diminish the fact they are powerful. There are a number of scriptures which can give us an idea of the power which is possessed by these ambassadors. As a representative of God, the angels were responsible to do the work of Jehovah in His stead.

II Peter 2:11, says "Whereas angels, which are greater in power and might, bring not railing accusation against them before the Lord."

Psalms 103:20 says "Bless the Lord, ye his angels, that excel in strength, that do his commandments, hearkening unto the voice of his word."

The angels are mighty but not almighty. Their power is delegated by God and we may seek His assistance to help us do His work. We find in II Thessalonians 1:7 that the angels are mighty in power. This power is available to the throne and as Children of God, those who have access to the throne room (Hebrews 4:16).

The work of <u>one angel</u>:

Smote the first born in Egypt: Psalms 78:51

Rolled back the stone at the tomb of Jesus: Mark 16: 4-6

Smote 185,000 Assyrians: Isaiah 37:36

Has the power to lay hold of Satan and bind him for 1000 years: Revelation 20:1-3.

Let us take notice of scriptures which show of the difference of rank in power as well as dignity. With the realization of their power and authority; the place each of these beings hold in our life adds dimension to our walk. The importance with which each holds to us as an individual can easily be understood.

Daniel 10:13; "But the prince of the kingdom of Persia withstood me one and twenty days: but, lo, Michael, one of the chief princes, came to help me; and I remained there with the kings of Persia."

Daniel 12:1; "And at that time shall Michael stand up, the great prince which standeth for the children of thy people: and there shall be a time of trouble, such as never was since there was a nation even to that same time: and at that time thy people shall be delivered, every one that shall be found written in the book."

I Thessalonians 4:16; "For the Lord himself shall descend from heaven with a shout, with the voice of the archangel, and with the trump of God: and the dead in Christ shall rise first:"

Jude 1:9; "Yet Michael the archangel, when contending with the devil he disputed about the body of Moses, durst not bring against him a railing accusation, but said, The Lord rebuke thee."

Colossians 1:16; "For by him were all things created, that are in heaven, and that are in earth, visible and invisible, whether they be thrones, or dominions, or principalities, or powers: all things were created by him, and for him:"

Angels not only have names given by God, but also have rank and order to their work. These "messengers" as translated from the Greek word "*angelos*" let us know the primary function of the angels in general is to serve as the messenger from God to the human race. Just as the designated position in military rank and order will explain the qualifications and responsibility, so also does their position give us an idea to the work of each particular member.

Mighty Angels, as in II Thessalonians 1:17 give us an insight to the power which these groups of warriors have for us to use. Another scripture found in Psalms 29:1; speaks of the "sons of the mighty" which are angels of great power. The term used – *Bene elim* or "sons of the mighty.

Watchers, as in Daniel 4:13,17; define angels as agents and overseers of God in the affairs of mankind. These angels make the heavens aware of what is going on in the presence of the saints of the Lord.

During a number of services which I attended while on the east coast, I was able to witness the "*watchers*" which God had sent to a local assembly. On two particular occasions while the choir was singing and the Spirit of the Lord was moving, I noticed an individual standing over against the wall. The person was not a member of the congregation and had never been. Everyone was in their seat or standing and clapping to the singing of the choir. The angel which was present was leaning up against the wall on the first occasion and standing stalwart on the second. As soon as I looked back to see him again, there was no one there. They are always around us and with us in the presence of the Lord.

Leitourgos (Greek) is a term used for angels which are servants and also those which minister.

Mishrathim (Hebrew) is a term used for angels which serve as servants and those who minister.

Host is used in the scripture for those who encompass the people of God and are members of the army of heaven. These are those who deliver messages (the birth of Jesus) and also fight to accomplish the will of the Lord. The Hebrew word for *host* is *sava.* (Ps. 33:6; 103:21; Lk. 2:13)

Sons of the mighty (Ps. 89:6)

The Elect (these will be covered in a separate chapter) (I Tim. 5:21)

Ministering Spirits (Heb. 1:14)

Seraphim (Isa. 6:1-7)

Cherubim (Gen. 3:24; Ezek. 1:5-28; 8:1-4; 10:1-22)

Archangels or chief angels who rule kingdoms and planets. (Col. 1:15-18; I Thess. 4:16; Jude 9)

Michael, one of the chief princes. (Dan. 10:13,21; 11:1; 12:1)

Gabriel, one who stands before God. (Dan. 8:16-19; 9:20-23; 10:8-11)

These "beings" have an important place and power available to be used by the born again believer. Each of these areas will be examined in greater detail as we take each area individually.

An Important Ministry

We do not know exactly when and where they were created, but anyone who reads the scripture must believe in these ministering spirits. The Bible speaks of them in very large numbers:

> (Daniel 7:10) "thousand thousands ministered unto him, and ten thousand times ten thousand stood before him: the judgment was set, and the books were opened."

> (Matthew 26:53) "Thinkest thou that I cannot now pray to my Father, and he shall presently give me more than twelve legions of angels?"

> (Luke 2:13) "And suddenly there was with the angel a multitude of the heavenly host praising God, and saying,"

> (Hebrews 12:22,23) "To the general assembly and church of the firstborn, which are written in heaven, and to God the Judge of all, and to the spirits of just men made perfect,"

(Revelation 5:11) "And I beheld, and I heard the voice of many angels round about the throne and the beasts and the elders: and the number of them was ten thousand times ten thousand, and thousands of thousands;"

Their name alone tells us of their importance. "ANGELS" - from the Hebrew "*malak*" means messenger or agent, which occurs about 150 times in the Old Testament. It occurs in both the singular and plural with approximately the same number of times in the New Testament where the translation from the Greek "*aggelos*" meaning messenger, agent, or minister.[1]

mal<aÆk, *mal-awk'*; from an unused root mean. to despatch as a deputy; *a messenger*; spec. of God, i.e. *an angel* (also a prophet, priest or teacher):—ambassador, angel, king, messenger.

mal<ak , "messenger; angel." In Ugaritic, Arabic, and Ethiopic, the verb le<ak means "to send." Even though *le<ak* does not exist in the Hebrew Old Testament, it is possible to recognize its etymological relationship to *mal<ak.* In addition, the Old Testament uses the word "message" in Hag. 1:13; this word incorporates the meaning of the root *le<ak*, "to send." Another noun form of the root is *mela<kah*, "work," which appears 167 times. The name Malachi—literally, "my messenger"—is based on the noun *mal<ak.*

> The noun *mal<ak* appears 213 times in the Hebrew Old Testament. Its frequency is especially great in the historical books, where it usually means "messenger".

These "messengers" sometimes were manifestations of the Divine presence of Jehovah in the Old Testament. Due to the frequency to these beings, one would most definitely have to agree to the importance which they hold. How could these heavenly manifestations be so numerous, powerful and available to the church and still not be used by the believer?

Let us examine a portion of scripture in Zechariah, chapter three. In this particular writing, a confrontation and conversation exist between (1) the angel of the Eternal, (2) Joshua, and (3) the Adversary. The Adversary is rebuked by the "angel of the Eternal" in verse 2; which is followed by the changing of the "dirty clothes" of Joshua and clean clothes as well as a clean turban are placed upon his head by the angel.

After the changing of the clothes from "dirty" ones to those of "state" – the angel of the Eternal says to him (Joshua) in verse 4; "See, I have made your iniquity pass from you." (Moffatt) The angel also makes a series of statements which this author finds very interesting; those which show the presence and power of each for us and to be made available to us.

> Zechariah, chapter 3 and verse 7; "The Lord of hosts declares that if you will follow my directions

> and do your duty to me, you shall rule my house and control my sacred courts, and I will give you the right of access to this company of mine."[2] (Moffatt)

How much more beautiful could this statement be? We must remember that this angel of the Eternal had previously "protested" (Zech 3:6 "And the angel of the Lord protested unto Joshua,") the fact that Joshua would not allow him to do that for which these ministering spirits were designed to do.

Their Role in The Church

Just as these angels, in their various roles of power and authority, can serve to aid the Kingdom of God as well as those who are born again of His Name and covered by His Blood—they can also serve as warriors for each of us. Many times in the scriptures - let us note - they have changed the course of history. There could be no better cause than of service to God and to work for Him; <u>the most noble of all causes.</u>

> As believers we journey to that city, going through a foreign land to meet our maker. Hebrews 11: 13; ". . and confessed that they were strangers and pilgrims on the earth."

On this journey we will come to pitfalls, confusing circumstances and decisions where Divine intervention will be required. The mission for which each of us has been called will require the help of "warriors" from the spiritual world. As the Apostle Paul would write, "I have fought a good fight, I have finished my course, I have kept the faith:" (II Timothy 4:7); let it not be overlooked that in his struggles of life and direction—the angels of the Lord was with him.

> Acts 27:23; "For there stood by me this night the angel of God, whose I am, and whom I serve,"

The angels played an important part in the ministry of Jesus Christ. From the very beginning until the end of His earthly time, the angels ministered unto Him. It would also be wise to take notice that Jesus never used the angels to circumvent the purpose for which He robed Himself in flesh. With the armies of heaven and all the power which Jesus Christ possessed, how easy it would have been to destroy iniquity and evil, to rid the world of all that was opposing to the Father's Will—only you and I would have become puppets to His purpose. The love which we have comes from the relationship of forgiveness and freedom to choose the right way to live. Although sin is a hard taskmaster, the will of man and the desires of man are honored by God. As I have chosen to live a life filled with His Spirit, one of dedication and consecration to the purpose and will of the Almighty; with it comes the armed forces from the military headquarters of the Almighty God.

As we have explored the angels, let us look briefly at places where they have served on behalf of the prophets. Just as the prophets were the voice of God to each particular period of time, we as the church are His voice to this generation. The angels have the same responsibility and ability to serve this generation as those previous.

> (I Kings 19:5) "And as he lay and slept under a juniper tree, behold, then an angel touched him, and said unto him, Arise and eat."

> (II Kings 6:17) "And Elisha prayed, and said, Lord, I pray thee, open his eyes, that he may see. And the Lord opened the eyes of the young man; and he saw: and, behold, the mountain was full of horses and chariots of fire round about Elisha."

> (Daniel 10:21) "But I will shew thee that which is noted in the scripture of truth: and there is none that holdeth with me in these things, but Michael your prince."

The Attributes of the Angels

The angels are very regimented and disciplined. As we look at the qualities which they possess, we can clearly understand their role in relationship to God. When looking at the facts about these beautiful, majestic creatures of heaven, it is then revealed to us their purpose for service to God and mankind.

1. Glorious (Luke 9:26)
2. Immortal (Luke 20:36)
3. Powerful (II Thess. 1:7; Rev. 18:1; Isa. 37:36)
4. Heavenly spirit beings (Ps. 104:4; Matt. 18:10; 22:30; Heb. 1:14)
5. Limited in knowledge (Mark 13:32)
6. Higher than man (Psalms 8:5)
7. Need no rest (Revelation 4:8)
8. Can appear visible and invisible (John. 20:12; Heb. 13:2)
9. Stand before God (II Chr. 18:18)
10. Speak (I Cor. 13:1)
11. Ascend and descend (Gen. 28:12; Jn. 1:51)
12. Created by Christ (Job 38:4-7; Ps. 148:2-5; Col. 1:16)
13. Are not to be worshipped (Col. 2:18)
14. Organized (Col. 1:16; 2:18; Rom. 8:38; Eph. 6:10-18)
15. Innumerable (Luke 2:13; Heb. 12:22)
16. To be judged (I Cor. 6:3)

17. Subject of God (Mt. 22:30)
18. Interested in earthly affairs (Luke 9:26; 15:7-10; I Tim. 5:21; I Pet. 1:12)
19. Desire the things of salvation (I Pet. 1:10-12)
20. Observe us (I Cor. 4:9)
21. Wear garments (John 20:12)
22. Appear unaware (Heb. 13:2)
23. Dwell in heaven (Rev. 12:12; 13:6)

Characteristics of the Father

Earlier we discussed how each of us has certain characteristics which we inherit from both our natural parents as well as the heavenly father. The angels were created by God; therefore they also will possess qualities which came from God.

1. Possess personal spirit bodies (Gen. 18:2,4,8; 19:1-22; Judg. 13:6)
2. Emotions (Luke 15:10)
3. Obedient (Rev. 12:2)
4. Desire (I Pet. 1:12)
5. Wisdom (Ez. 28:17)

6. Anointed (Ez. 28:14)

7. Pride (Ez. 27:17)

8. Meekness (Jude 9; II Pet. 2:11)

9. Patience (Numbers 22:22-35)

10. Modest (I Cor. 11:10)

11. Holy (Mk. 8:38)

12. Will Power (Isa. 14: 12-14)

In the following chapters we will explore the place of these beautiful creatures in the life of Jesus Christ, the heirs of salvation and their relationship to salvation. Just as God seeks men to do His work on the earth, the angels are sent forth with instructions to give men and aid the completion of such work. The "armored" brigade which has been sent from the glory world will not step out of place or usurp the authority given them by their maker. Just as we desire to be in step with God, we cannot promote our personal agenda with the army of God. When using them (they are for our use), we must make sure we ask direction and know where we are headed.

"And when forty years were expired, there appeared to him in the wilderness of mount Sina an angel of the Lord in a flame of fire in a bush.

When Moses saw it, he wondered at the sight: and as he drew near to behold it, the voice of the Lord came unto him,

Saying, I am the God of thy fathers, the God of Abraham, and the God of Isaac, and the God of Jacob. Then Moses trembled, and durst not behold.

Then said the Lord to him, Put off thy shoes from thy feet: for the place where thou standest is holy ground.

I have seen, I have seen the affliction of my people which is in Egypt, and I have heard their groaning, and am come down to deliver them. And now come, I will send thee into Egypt.

This Moses whom they refused, saying, Who made thee a ruler and a judge? the same did God send to be a ruler and a deliverer by the hand of the angel which appeared to him in the bush. He brought them out, after that he had shewed wonders and signs in the land of Egypt, and in the Red sea, and in the wilderness forty years.

This is that Moses, which said unto the children of Israel, A prophet shall the Lord your God raise up unto you of your brethren, like unto me; him shall ye hear.

This is he, that was in the church in the wilderness with the angel which spake to him in the mount Sinai, and with our fathers: who received the lively oracles to give unto us:"

Acts 7: 30-38

Mighty Angels

"And he said, Hear thou therefore the word of the Lord: I saw the Lord sitting on his throne, and all the host of heaven standing by him on his right hand and on his left.

I Kings 19:22

Chapter Two

The Mighty Angels

"And to you who are troubled rest with us, when the Lord Jesus shall be revealed from heaven with his mighty angels," (KJV)

"And to (recompense) you who are so distressed and afflicted (by granting you) relief and rest along with us (your fellow sufferers) when the Lord Jesus is revealed from heaven with His mighty angels in a flame of fire," (AMP)

Although all the angels are powerful, the "Mighty Angels" are the warriors of God to which we have access in a walk of victory. From the beginning of man's seeking for direction in the life of Abraham until today, we would be wise to accept these fighters to wage war against the adversary of our soul and the Kingdom of God.

> Matthew 11:12; ". . .until now the kingdom of heaven suffereth violence, and the violent take it by force."

Since the time of the Garden of Eden and the existence of man, Satan has waged war against all which is associated with God. Since his removal from the heavens (Isaiah 14:12), there has been a war and will be until the end when Satan is bound by the angel and cast into the pit for one thousand years (Revelation 20:1-3). As we read and study the epistles; which were written to the born again believer, it becomes very evident of the spiritual war each of us have become involved in.

> II Timothy 2:4; "No man that warreth entangleth himself with the affairs of this life; that he may please him who hath chosen him to be a soldier."

We are reminded that the warfare is not carnal and understanding to the human mind. Just as it will be fought in the spiritual realm—we need the spiritual warriors (God's military machine) to give us their help. As long as we seek the mind and will of God, the victory will be assured. When I get out of His will to pursue mine, then I am on my own and can expect anything to happen—you may rest assured that it will (I Corinthians 10:12).

"Wherefore let him that thinketh he standeth take heed lest he fall."

Protection

When military forces are spoken of in modern society and training methods are evaluated; a subject which is included is the ability to offer protection. As those who have been purchased by the blood of Calvary and born of the spirit, we have the constant protection of the angels.

> Psalms 34:7, "The angel of the Lord encampeth round about them that fear him, and delivereth them."
>
> Psalms 91:11, "For he shall give his angels charge over thee, to keep thee in all thy ways."

Not only are we saved from ourselves, sin and the devil; but we have the constant protection of the power of God in our life. The beauty of a Christian life and its separation from sin includes the keeping power. Knowing I do not have to worry for what might happen, the assurance of the hand of God and His angels offers a peace which cannot be measured. The angels of God are there before you are, they have already made a path for you to walk in and following in His steps should be your only concern.

> Psalms 57:3; "He shall send from heaven, and save me from the reproach of him that would swallow me up. . ."

Psalms 40:11; ". . let thy lovingkindness and thy truth continually preserve me."

In the Old Testament, an awesome sight is seen with one great military leader having a meeting with "another." A great military commander for the Israelites (Joshua) has come by Jericho, "that he lifted up his eyes and looked, and, behold, there stood a man over against him with his sword drawn in his hand;" (Joshua 5:13-15). When Joshua gets to Jericho, the angel (warrior, commander) of the Lord was already there. What a joy can be found when we know that the angels of the Lord are with us wherever we go and also before we get there; God cares enough to send His angelic forces to lead us to victory.

Another example is found in a battle with the Assyrians in the Second Book of the Kings. Elisha and his servant are hiding in the city of Dothan. When the servant had awakened the next morning, the city had been surrounded by the enemies. A very famous scripture came out of this adverse situation when the servant turned to Elisha and asked the question "Alas, my master! how shall we do?" (II Kings 6:15).

How often have we faced the same situation, or even asked the identical question? It is in this type of dilemma the true nature of the angels can be made known. How else would one know He can heal, unless we would get sick? How else would we know he can supply our needs, unless we were short changed and had needs? The greatest blessing we can have is the comfort of knowing we are in His hands and He cares for us.

After the question by his servant, Elisha prayed and the Lord answered—as He will when we seek His will and direction. As the words of the Hebrew children to the king, "our God is able to deliver us. . "(Daniel 3:17) We find the Lord gave the servant what he needed; just as He will give us what we need in a time of distress.

> II Kings 6:17; "And Elisha prayed, and said, Lord, I pray thee, open his eyes, that he may see. And the Lord opened the eyes of the young man; and he saw: and, behold, the mountain was full of horses and chariots of fire round about Elisha."
>
> Psalms 34:7; "The angel of the Lord encampeth round about them that fear him, and delivereth them."
>
> Psalms 91:15; "He shall call upon me, and I will answer him: I will be with him in trouble; I will deliver him, and honour him."

We are not always to know what to do, except to call "upon the name of the Lord" and He will supply our needs. As those who see with the natural eye, the things of the spirit will not be understood. Our dependence upon God will give direction to the pathway which we should travel. Just because we cannot see the ministering spirits does not mean they are not there; the spiritual are only seen with spiritual vision.

Offensive Angels

When it is needed and a requirement in our life, we are glad for the protection given to the heirs of salvation. Protection all the time is not that positive, should we spend all our time in this “mode” - it will become a defensive position. A military group of any quality at all must find the attack form to “force its will” upon the enemy. What greater enemy is there than the one which stalks our soul. Jesus said, “but rather fear him which is able to destroy both soul and body in hell.” (Matthew 10:28).

Just as the enemy will not rest or sleep from the onslaught on the Kingdom of God; we cannot let up for one moment to continually fight for the truth and lives of those who need us. The responsibility (command) of each believer has always been to declare war on the kingdom of our adversary. If we will take this battle to Satan and all he represents, then the mighty commanders and warriors of the Lord will assist us to victory. All the victories anyone will see depend upon the continued faith in God.

We can find examples of this in the Old Testament. When Jehovah had promised the children of Israel the land which was theirs, He provided a way for them to see the victory. When we have the Word of God, then we can be guaranteed the victory.

> Exodus 33:2; "And I will send an angel before thee; and I will drive out the Canaanite, the Amorite, and the Hittite, and the Perizzite, the Hivite, and the Jebusite:"

Seeking the warrior angels will prove to be an advantage for each individual in the conquest to destroy Satan. Whether it is to bind the Prince of a city, place an angel as protection or send revelation of salvation to someone who is lost - the mighty angels are at the available service from God's throne. One such event took place in the Acts of the Apostles. The Christian Church was being destroyed by a "religious" leader who thought he was doing what was right. After much approved destruction, the Church began to **pray** that God would intercede for them. After much prayer (a petition or request) the single most spoken about event took place. Notice how the warriors of the Lord answered the prayer for the Church.

> Acts 9:3, "And as he journeyed, he came near Damascus: and suddenly there shined round about him a light from heaven:"

> Acts 9:4, "And he fell to the earth, and heard a voice saying unto him, Saul, Saul, why persecutest thou me?"

I remember one morning at approximately four a.m., a most awesome sight was shown to me from God in prayer. At that particular time, I was praying the third watch and had been doing this schedule for about three weeks. As I was praying, there seemed to be an uncontrollable burden which consumed me. As I began to pray, the burden of travail brought to mind a particular family and prayer was made for them. (I did not even talk to this family, let alone the fact that I would have the vaguest idea of the problem they were going through.) After a period of time, I got up off the floor and began to walk around and pray when it seemed the roof opened up toward the heavens. As I looked up, there seeming to "fall" or "leap" from heaven was an angel with a flaming sword. It was a flaming victory for this particular family. After contact with the family the next morning, I discovered that God was answering a prayer.

> Revelation 10:1; "And I saw another mighty angel come down from heaven, clothed with a cloud: and a rainbow was upon his head, and his face was as it were the sun, and his feet as pillars of fire:"

One example of the need for a warrior angel came in a series of meetings which were being held in an East Texas community. Having been there for the second time, many found the more awesome demonstrations of God to be some what questionable to say the least. (There comes a time when the mighty angels are needed to bind spirits and allow God to move as His will would desire.) In an early prayer session one morning, while praying for the session that evening (this meeting was on prayer and fasting), I saw the vision of a snake crawl in from the platform into the audience and to a particular seat. The snake came from a particular place on the platform. At the end of the service on prayer, all who desired came for prayer to the altar. At the end of the service, the snake was brought to existence. The devil was cast out of the lady, God had delivered her and He would receive the glory for it.

Binding the Workplace

Karen had worked for a major Louisiana insurance company for the past ten years until her retirement. During her last year as the receptionist for the company, each morning would bring the most fearful as well as binding feelings when she would arise in preparation for work. Almost instantly each morning when the alarm clock would sound, a spirit of fear and depression would consume her and cause her to weep from the thought of having to go to the office.

While working in my office in Denham Springs, Louisiana; I felt to give her a call (unaware of what had been going on) and see how the day was going. When she answered the phone, I immediately knew something was not right. She informed me that she was in the process of running away to some place where no one would find her. It was this call which stirred her back to reality of how bad the problem had become. I asked her to do nothing until we could talk about it that evening when I got home.

In our discussion, she then revealed to me how every morning when she awoke that she would cry in the shower, dreading to even drive to the office. This situation had become too bad to ignore and we both realized that we needed help from the angels of the Lord.

Drawing from the book of Exodus, we followed the example of the scripture when Moses instructed the Children of Israel to put the blood over the door post and on the lintels (Exodus 12:7-24). The next morning I gave her some prayerful instructions as what to do when she got to work.

Getting up very early the next morning, Karen was excited to go to the office. The thrill had nothing to do with going to work, but rather what the Lord was going to do for her that day. As the vehicle turned to drive in the parking lot, she uttered a very simple phrase, "I bind every spirit of the adversary which would come against me today in the Name of Jesus and cover this parking lot with the power of the blood of Jesus."

Upon placing the key in the lock, she uttered the very same phrase and bound every spirit which would come against her. As the door closed behind her, she proceeded to visit the foyer and all seventeen other rooms and offices; binding the spirits which would come from each and commanding them to be defeated.

Sometime during the morning hours was when I received a call from her to let me know how great work was going. Nothing could bother her and every time someone or something would try to hinder her, she would rebuke it under her breath and the attitude would cease.

Once again, the power which we have been given was used for the protection and possibly the sanity of the born again believer.

If we fail to use the Mighty Angels—we loose the advantages we were meant to have.

Sending Them Forth

What good does it do when there are the angelic servants of God waiting to serve me and I simply ignore them? Our time in prayer can be made in a very simple statement: it is worship that includes all the attitudes of the human spirit in its approach to God. The Christian worships God when he adores, confesses, praises and comes in supplication to Him in prayer. This is the highest activity of which the human spirit is capable of doing. The very power of our communion with God is found in prayer.

> "God is a Spirit: and they that worship him must worship him in spirit and in truth." John 4:24

Prayer is the character of God; the necessity of a man's saving relationship or covenant relationship when entering in fully into all the privileges and obligations from heaven. With every man coming into a covenant with God, the agreement is returned; in which we have access to the angels of His mighty army.

> "Verily I say unto you, Whatsoever ye shall bind on earth shall be bound in heaven: and whatsoever ye shall loose on earth shall be loosed in heaven." Matthew 18:18

While I am on my knees in prayer, I have discovered this scripture to be true. At the entrance to the throne of God, the communion time with Him when there are absolutely no others around to discourage you—the petitions to God are made and bound. In order to understand them, we must first know them. No human on earth can explain a step by step process; this comes only with activities which are done with God as your partner.

It is told that many years ago, the Satanist of South Africa fasted for approximately forty days. During this time of the fast to their leader, (the adversary of our soul) only one request was made. This request was simply: "Destroy the marriages of Christian Leaders." So great was their concentrated effort, and marriages were destroyed, many families broken and all types of sin began to invade the ministry and its leaders. If these who serve evil could dedicate themselves for their cause; it is far more noble for those who have been washed in the blood of Jesus Christ to use the armies He has provided.

> "Who maketh his angels spirits; his ministers a flaming fire:" Psalms 104:4

> "Praise ye him, all his angels: praise ye him, all his hosts." Psalms 148:2

In looking at the Old Testament events in the life of Joshua which shows the angels of God wait upon us to request them. The events of Zechariah 3:1-8 gives a discourse with the Lord and Satan in the presence of Joshua. In this conversation the clothing of Joshua is changed, filthy garments are changed for the pure clothing. Notice the phrase of the angel in verse 6 and the reason for it in the following verse.

> "And the angel of the Lord protested unto Joshua, saying," Zechariah 3:6

> " I will give thee places to walk among these that stand by." Zechariah 3:7

They stand in place, waiting upon us to call for them. When we do not use them—then they become "upset." The angels; those who serve in the courts of heaven for all the blood bought heirs; "protest" when they are not allowed to function for the glory of God.

Use them and victory is assured by Heaven!

While living in Central Louisiana, I received a call from a frantic lady that her mother had been in a horrible accident and was taken to the intensive care unit at the hospital. The doctor had told the family she probably would not live and if she did, there would be permanent damage since her brain had begun to swell. The family was beside themselves to say the least and in very much disarray. I began to pray with her over the phone, we commanded the angels of healing to go into the intensive ward and bind the swelling in the Name of Jesus and to cover her with His Blood. We agreed and believed the healing was already completed. (It is important when entering the spirit world that each time you send the angels and the power of the Name of Jesus that you truly believe it – if you do not, nothing will happen.)

The next morning, I received another call from the same "frantic" lady. The doctor was amazed at the condition of her sister. The brain had ceased to swell and everything was functioning normally. The sister went home about a week later.

When Jesus was approached in the gospels about the centurion having a sick daughter, he sent his healing power to do the work. The Bible says that "the same hour" the girl began to mend. (Matthew 8:8-10)

In the book of Acts, we can read the account of the Apostle Peter in the prison. The scripture tells us that the church began to pray. While the church was praying, the angel of the Lord freed the Apostle and led him to the street so that he could go on his way. While the church was still praying, the Apostle knocked on the door. (Acts 12:1-6)

"The angel of the Lord encampeth round about them that fear him, and delivereth them."

Psalms 34: 7

"Take heed that ye despise not one of these little ones; for I say unto you, That in heaven their angels do always behold the face of my Father which is in heaven."

Matthew 18:10

Guardian Angels

"I saw in the visions of my head upon my bed, and, behold, a watcher and an holy one came down from heaven;"

Daniel 7:9

Chapter Thee

Guardian Angels

Most likely the Guardian Angels are the ones which each of us relate to. This angel, from the heart of the artist to the canvas, has been given the greatest amount of publicity. These ministering spirits are a vital part of each of us and probably the one which gives the most satisfaction in the Christian adventure.

In a world filled with chaos, hatred, frustrations and general confusion; there is nothing but excited feelings when knowing beyond a doubt that the angels of heaven are there to protect.

> Luke 22:43; "And there appeared an angel unto him from heaven, strengthening him."
>
> Psalms 34:7; "The angel of the Lord encampeth round about them that fear him, and delivereth them."

The old cliché, "royalty has its advantages" holds more weight than one can possibly imagine. A family that lives behind the enclosed walls and large gates of modern society are often envied because of what is hidden from the view of a general public. How shocking it sometimes can be to find a life in ruins and discord, knowing there was nothing to stop the success but those who lived there. The same can be said of the spiritual world that a believer lives in.

According to the scriptures, we are a royal priesthood (I Peter 2:9) and the advantages of this classification were included in our redemption. An individual who has been raised or adopted by a royal family never question the benefits which are present nor future. In the writings to the Church in the first epistle from Peter, we are reminded, "cast your cares upon him; for he careth for you." (I Peter 5:7). Why would those who live in such a position of excellence and prestige need to be reminded?

When the born again believer has been adopted (Romans 8:15) into the family of God, all the benefits come with it. There were no exclusions to this contract which would leave or give more privileges to another. In fact, just the opposite is true. The next verse (vs. 16) calls each of us *"the children of God"* and oh, how we love our children. The focus of our existence, and that which has gotten many in trouble, is often because of their offspring.

As a member (even if by adoption) of the royal family, all the powers of heaven are at my disposal. As long as we remain in the family, by obedience to the Word of God, each one has the entire royal courts of heaven standing at attention. Every time I speak the Name of Jesus, all of heaven and earth wait for my hearts desire.

Father Relationships

As with any child and their father, the ongoing relationship is very important. This constant understanding is maintained by daily communication and contact. It is easy to say the words - "I Love You" - but to fulfill the strength of this small phrase can be another event altogether. I enjoy talking to my children as often as possible; it is the sound of their voice, knowing their needs as well as their joys are important to me. One cannot say that we *love* if the action does not verify the same.

If we love someone, we will make every effort to communicate with them. The longest time period in my life was when my oldest daughter was not accessible to me. During a four month span, she labored for the Lord, overseas in a mission work - I could not call or hear the sound of her voice. These months would seem like an eternity, a forever which would not end. With my two daughters which live at home and myself being a number of states away involved in the work of the Lord; I will often call and leave a message on the answering machine or drop a simple card to remind them—they are on my heart and mind.

How can we say we love our Heavenly Father, except we talk to Him? An understanding of the Courts of Heaven, how the benefits of adoption can apply to the life of the believer, and knowing when God speaks to us; all are dependent upon our communication with Him. Our prayer time is where we hear His voice and can have the reassurance of the relationship between us and the one who died for humanity.

Take notice of the fact that when prayer is mentioned, the voice of God is required for an understanding. So often we play "tag" with God; almost as if to touch Him and say "you're it." We need to spend time with Him - a good relationship requires at least two parties with the same objectives. God is interested in knowing my needs, and He will supply them (Philippians 4:19); but I must know His Will, direction and purpose in my life.

> Philippians 4:6 "Be careful for nothing; but in every thing by prayer and supplication with thanksgiving let your requests be made known unto God."

The Guardian Angels are part of the family of Heaven. As I remain close to God, His angels will be there constantly to protect me. A member of a royal family does not have to request an escort - it is part of the family benefits. It would be quite surprising if at some point in life I found out the President of the United States had to fill out a requisition order for the services of protection. The same is true with a child of God, though the President is important in the natural realm (I wish to take nothing away from this office or the man), the most important arena of our life is the eternal realm - the spiritual.

A number of years ago, I was working for a very large corporation. Being involved in contracts, they desired and would get a lot of my time and wanted more. It seemed my family life and more importantly my spiritual life was left in limbo, which is another way to say it was actually going downhill. One day in prayer, the Lord spoke to me about leaving this lucrative money making position since its demands took all I had. Knowing I had heard from God made the decision a little easier; but the natural mind did think about the financial side and possible effects.

Standing one morning in the presence of the Almighty, without a job or where I would go next; knowing that my oldest daughter would be getting married and that would not be cheap - still I knew what had been done was in His perfect will. With my arms still hanging at my side and bent ever so slightly at the elbows toward the heavens, I was basking in the awesome presence of my Father. There are many things which can be said about being in the presence of Jehovah; alone with Him will bring satisfaction that words cannot explain and a peace that is genuine.

While lost in this state of mind in an earthly sense, I was much alive in the spiritual. I felt what I thought was a person behind me giving a reassurance to one who has stepped out on the **voice of God** in pure faith. I physically felt a hand slip between my arm pit and rib, slide itself down to my elbow and make its way up my arm to my open palms. As the hand reached my palms it slid into my fingers and took the most positive hold I have ever felt in my life. A warmness completely overtook me and I turned to my left to give a reassurance to the friend who from behind was offering a comfort.

The Angel of God

I looked at a blank wall, nothing was there that could be seen with human eyes. At that instant a voice spoke to me in my left ear. I can still hear the voice today, the words ring ever so clear; *Take hold of my hand, I will lead you and take care of you. Everything will be alright.* In the months that followed this encounter with my angel, I would try to worry (a human trait) and the voice of the Lord would ask me why worry since He had all of my circumstances in control. My oldest daughter was married in a beautiful ceremony, there were those who saw the angels of the Lord lined around the sanctuary and every need was supplied.

These ministering spirits are not some spooky attitude, an expression of a desire; but real and vibrant spirits from the throne of God. Though a spirit does not have a body, nevertheless they do exist and are real. Through prayer and pure service unto God; there are advantages in the Kingdom.

> Zechariah 9:8 "And I will encamp about mine house because of the army, because of him that passeth by, and because of him that returneth: and no oppressor shall pass through them any more: for now have I seen with mine eyes."

It was the Sunday evening before school would start the following day. My daughter would start to school the next morning, and along with her mother, this was the scheduled time to meet those who would have a part in her life for the next year. When we stepped from the automobile and made our way to the battle field where my "little girl" would wrestle with evil for the next nine months, here I realized the need of my petition to God for the angels to intercede.

I remember the horror that grasp my heart, the fear which tried to possess me. As we walked through the school, I would command the angels of protection to guard every door she would walk through, I even sent angels to stand guard over her locker and at the doors where she would hold class. At one point I filled the gym and cafeteria with angels over her.

> St. John 14:14; "If ye shall ask any thing in my name, I will do it."

Driving away from the school, I commented aloud of how I could not believe that "I" would leave my daughter to these wolves. It was here that the Lord spoke to my spirit about dispatching His angels to do the work. My daughter had a great year, lived an excellent example of Christianity and what living for Jesus Christ is all about. (We can invoke the powers of our Father who has a great love for us.)

The Family

Since the Lord led Abraham out of the land of his fathers, He has always kept the covenant which He made. As would any earthly father do, the heavenly father (Matthew 7:11) desires that His family be taken care of. The promises of God have not lost any integrity nor strength, they will never diminish and are the only true promises which will never fail. If we will be faithful and just - then He will take care of us.

> Psalms 119:137 "Righteous art thou, O Lord, and upright are thy judgments."
>
> Psalms 119:138 "Thy testimonies that thou hast commanded are righteous and very faithful."

Though there are too many to name them all, let us look at an example from the scriptures of the guardian angel of the Lord protecting a member of the family.

When there is faithfulness toward God, then He will return the same unto us. This relationship was not only purchased with the blood at Calvary, but must be maintained with trust and faithfulness by our service and submission to Him.

A servant of God had committed to pray three times a day, lift his heart and eyes toward Jerusalem even living in a strange land. Because of this commitment to Jehovah, even in trying circumstances, the Lord blessed him and brought favor to his life. In the favor from Jehovah, Darius set Daniel over the princes; how ironic that a heathen king would place a vessel of Jehovah over a heathen land.

When jealousy arose, a formal decree resulted and because of his commitment to Jehovah; his sentence was to die in the den of lions. Let us take notice that when the judgment was handed down, it was not Daniel who did not sleep that night—it was the king who had signed the decree in error. Daniel 6:18 tells us ". . .and his sleep went from him." We never have to fear when living for the Lord is sincere. Take notice of the verse in which Daniel, who was faithful, acknowledges the guardian angel of Jehovah in his life.

> Daniel 6:22; "My God hath sent his angel, and hath shut the lions' mouths, that they have not hurt me: "

As we close this chapter on the guardian angels, let us recall the scripture which informs us that the children have their own “personal” angel. But not only in the fact that “children” as the little ones who run around the house with socks and shoes missing or cheeks with chocolate on them; we are the *children of the most high God.*

> Matthew 18:10; “Take heed that ye despise not one of these little ones; for I say unto you, That in heaven their angels do always behold the face of my Father which is in heaven.”

Not to be redundant or repeat myself due to the lack of words, for the scriptures are filled with the ministering of these angels and our accessibility to them. We may seek His face, His will, His favor and direction—then we are assured of the ministering angels, whether they are protectors or warfare angels.

I was headed on a nine hundred mile trip, one which does not bring an extreme amount of excitement. Knowing I was in the mind of God and doing what was right brought a peace to me as well as the excitement that is found with new expectations in God. Driving a U-haul with a vehicle in tow, I must admit it was not very smart driving at the rate of speed which I was keeping. Singing my way through every state, talking to the Lord (my unseen companion) along the way was the most exciting part of the travel.

For some reason, as I neared my destination, I could not help but think how easy this trip had gone. There was such a feeling of the presence of God and the angels of the Most High with me the whole time. Upon arrival to my final destination, the time came for the unloading of the u-haul. I went back to unhook the vehicle in tow, and the sight which I looked upon made me shutter.

Having gone down the road at excessive speed, moving down the interstate with reckless abandon and only God on my mind; my thoughts never reflected that the automobile I was pulling had become unhooked. At what point I do not know, for how many miles I am not sure; the only fact for which I can be positive is the angel of thc Lord was there and I felt it for a purpose.

Someday we will all arrive at our destination - the final one. Let us make sure the angels of the Lord are there with us and we have felt His guidance the whole way.

Do-Do's Angel

Since two of our grandchildren live about ten hours away, there are long stretches of time in which we are not able to visit or spend time with them. Karen and I have made it a point of emphasis to have them come and spend from two weeks to a month with us in order to enjoy their growing years. These times have offered some exciting and rewarding experiences for us as grandparents.

Lyric, the older of the two, has a unique personality for a three year old. When conversing with others, he will speak of himself in the third person while throwing his hands upward with palms open in order to emphasize the importance of what he is saying. In their last visit, he would continue to tell his "Ganny" (as he calls her), "Do-Do is happy."

After the first week, we were convinced that he was happy and came to realize the reason for it during the middle of the second. One morning early, Karen woke up and looked over to the bed where our grandson was peacefully sleeping and noticed an additional occupant in the room. There standing at the head of the bed where "Do-Do" was sleeping stood an angel guarding over him.

In a home where there is peacefulness and harmony, we should not find it strange to have the visitation of angels – in fact; we should seek for the divine guidance of God in our daily lives.

"And, behold, there was a great earthquake: for the angel of the Lord descended from heaven, and came and rolled back the stone from the door, and sat upon it.

His countenance was like lightning, and his raiment white as snow:

And for fear of him the keepers did shake, and became as dead men.

And the angel answered and said unto the women, Fear not ye: for I know that ye seek Jesus, which was crucified.

He is not here: for he is risen, as he said. Come, see the place where the Lord lay.

And go quickly, and tell his disciples that he is risen from the dead; and, behold, he goeth before you into Galilee; there shall ye see him: lo, I have told ."

Matthew 28:2-7

Ministering Angels

"Forasmuch as ye are manifestly declared to be the epistle of Christ ministered by us, written not with ink, but with the Spirit of the living God; not in tables of stone, but in fleshy tables of the heart."

II Corinthians 3:3

Chapter Four

Ministering Angels

There could not be a better way, other than the offering of Himself at Calvary for the sins of mankind—to express His love for the Church. Not only did the King of Glory leave the splendor of His royal palace and visit the sinful land of man where turmoil, aggravation, and all that is distasteful dwell; but He also has given the angels for our use. Those who were originally created to give worship and honor daily to him (Isaiah 6:2-3); now also aid those who are of the Family of God.

It is a war that wages in far more than the natural arena; the angels of God are there to see that the purpose and will of "him who hath called you out of this darkness" (I Peter 2:9) will be accomplished. Since the promise of God was given to Adam and Eve in the Garden of Eden, a war has been declared for rule of man's soul.

> Genesis 3:15 "And I will put enmity between thee and the woman, and between thy seed and her seed; it shall bruise thy head, and thou shalt bruise his heel."

Not only did God manifest Himself in the flesh (Colossians 2:9) and give His life up on Calvary (St. John 10:17), but has also made the ministering angels of service to the royal family. These angels have played an important part in the ministry of Jesus Christ as well as the church. From the times since the call of Abraham until today, they are ever present.

As children of the Most High God, there are angels who are to minister to our needs. When there are needs present, these angels are there to assist us in our challenges of life; when there are those who have needs, we can invoke the rights of the family and send these angels to those who are in distress. How often have Christians been left shortchanged because we have not understood all which is available to each and every born again believer?

> Psalms 91:11; "For he shall give his angels charge over thee, to keep thee in all thy ways."

Angels in Attendance

They were twin cities filled with lust, perversion, obscene lifestyles, vile addictions and rape. Anything evil was prevalent in Sodom and Gomorrah, the very place where a relative of the father of the faithful would live. As so often in our life, decisions we make may not be those which can end up as the landmark of choices. Lot had taken his family to what would end up the most despicable place on the face of the earth. God was intending to destroy these two cities since the iniquity had become so great.

The Lord spoke to Abraham (Genesis 18:17-19) of the decision which He had made to destroy Sodom and Gomorrah. As Abraham spoke with Jehovah, he pleaded for the redemption of this city. Because of the conversations between Abraham and Jehovah, and the fact that the number of righteous cannot be found - Sodom and Gomorrah was to be destroyed.

Because of the righteousness of Abraham, the ministering angels made numerous visits to Lot and would take them out of a city so filled with sin. It is these angels which are called to minister or "to serve" us today. Let us not only use them but let us send them forth that others can be blessed.

> Psalms 91:12 "They shall bear thee up in their hands, lest thou dash thy foot against a stone."

As these angels are for the needs of the saints, most commonly it would lend to spiritual, financial and those who are supporting the cause of Jesus Christ in action. Often times in doing the work to deliver the souls of mankind, since the work is of a spiritual nature—the physical body will become exhausted.

In the Old Testament book of I Kings, one of the most phenomenal victories had been given for Jehovah. Elijah has delivered a victory for the children of Israel, the prophets of Baal have been defeated and Jezebel is very wroth. The rain which had been stopped by the Prophet Elijah will now begin because of his prayers. All of this seems like there would be a cause for untold celebration in the land, but this does not happen.

Having been threatened by Jezebel, Elijah flees to Beer-sheba and sits down to rest under a juniper tree (I Kings 19:4). Because the journey ahead of him is long and there is much work to be done, the angel comes and awakens him to eat a meal which he (the angel) has prepared (I Kings 19:5-8).

Ministering to Missionaries

Those who go on a journey for the cause of the gospel are often left in a place of loneliness, a place where the divine messengers of God will be. We can find a number of these examples in the New Testament to give us the encouragement and assurance that God is faithful to His own. It does not matter how, nor are the heavens bound by our finite dimensions and thought boundaries, God has, can and will move for a member of His family.

It has not been discussed before this point, but there are visitations of God which will use that of a human being. There have been the "visitors" which do the work of the Lord, someone who has never been seen and will never be seen again. It this chapter, the angels we are talking about minister to the need of the saints and the situations are often answered by entertaining the unknown.

> Hebrews 13:2 "Be not forgetful to entertain strangers: for thereby some have entertained angels unawares."

In the New Testament, we find the apostles doing the work for which they had been called. As usually is the case when men are moved by the power of God, others are convicted and stirred. The apostle Peter was ministering the word and power of God and those of the "religious" community became upset and had him thrown in prison. It was the opinion of this "sect of the Sadducees" (Acts 5:17), because of their jealousy that he should be imprisoned. After such an act, the angel of the Lord came and set him free from the chains that bound him. Once again the missionary work would not be hindered by the spirits of man.

After Herod had killed James the brother of John (Acts 12:2), he felt this act brought joy to the Jews. In a more blatant act, he had the apostle Peter arrested and put into prison. His intentions were to keep him there, but once again the angel of the Lord set him free. When the word is used, the motives are pure and our objectives are His kingdom and not our own; then the angels of the Lord will be sent to give us the aid we need.

Personal Manifestations

> Luke 12:32 "Fear not, little flock; for it is your Father's good pleasure to give you the kingdom."

Should it not be an expectation from all born again believers: if the Jehovah of the Old Testament, those of the children of Israel, the children of Abraham, Isaac and Jacob be taken care of then He will take care of His blood purchased church. Those who were assisted in the beginning can serve as an example (I Corinthians 10:11) of what is desired for the royal priesthood today.

Please allow me to re-emphasize the fact (not to be repetitious) of extreme importance, all directives, understandings, visitations from God as well as messengers will only come when our will is lost in His will. To seek the mind of God we must be very unselfish and to promote His purpose has to be without reservation. The reason those in the bible were called disciples was because they promoted the will of the one whom they followed. A disciple is one who has enough discipline to forsake personal plans, lay them aside for a greater cause.

One morning after a prayer session, a time alone at home with God; the presence of His power was as peaceful and comforting as one could ever dream. Before I go any further, let me explain some terminology which I have acquired in reference to my prayer life. When this author speaks of times "at home" in prayer; these are not locations such as a building or even a particular room. There is nothing physical about being at home. Home in this sense is a place where I am with God. My soul and all that is within me is at "home" with Him who made me and washed my sin with His blood.

After a few hours of prayer, I had begun to meditate and listen for the voice of God to speak to me. It is essential that I hear from Him, my directions will go astray without the proper leading from Him. Even the best times in prayer cannot be termed a "success" if I have not gotten directions from the master of my soul. As I sat there in silence, my soul began to listen for the voice so familiar to give me what I needed. I could hear the angels walking around in my presence; in fact it was so vivid that it was like I could even hear the freshness of their breath.

It was in this hallowed presence of the King of Kings that the Lord spoke to me of a loneliness that I would be moved into; but the rewards would be of untold value. A few weeks later, a lady who has an anointing of God became a messenger to reaffirm what had been spoken to me. She would speak of the loneliness which would transcend into my life, the ministry that no individual would seek. Often, while driving down the road or in the long hours of the night - an empty feeling will come and I am reminded of the confirmation from the messenger which God sent to me.

The ministering angels are for all who will seek a place in the court of heaven. In His presence is the only place where peace, joy and happiness can ever exist.

> Romans 14:17 "For the kingdom of God is not meat and drink; but righteousness, and peace, and joy . . ."

You Will Know by the Feel

I recently visited a lady who had an antique shop, since these items of days past offer a bit of intrigue for me; it is an era I know little or nothing about. It was during this visit that the following story was related to me; one which could also be applied to the spiritual sense.

As her husband went on a hunting trip near Montgomery, Texas; she would often shop around to pass the time they were there. Outside of Montgomery, lived a little German lady named Mrs. Winslow—an antique specialist. Her shop was filled with all types of items from past days of history which she would ship to America from Europe every year.

Having a keen interest and wanting to go into business for herself, Shirley asked the owner which book and information she would recommend. With a quick twirl, throwing her arms in the air with frustration; Mrs. Winslow made a most remarkable statement - "You need no book, it comes with the feel."

This remarkable lady could pick up a piece of silver and tell if it was real or an imitation. With careful, sensitive fingers she would rub a sterling plate and tell you what the metal was underneath the outer shell. When she was handed a porcelain cup or bowl, without ever turning it over she could tell the year it was made.

When asked how she could do it, her simple reply was with a smile—"you have to experience antiques." In living for God and walking with Him in prayer; it has to be a living experience. When we "live" and "experience" the ministry of the angels, a victory is assured.

The Work of the Angels

As we take a quick overview, we can see the work of the "ministering spirits" which are available for every child of God. Their jobs are specific and each has the discipline from which God made them with – to fulfill His will for mankind.

1. Guard the gates (Rev. 21:12)
2. Bind Satan (Rev. 20)
3. Minister before God (Rev. 8:2; 14:7-10)
4. Minister to the saints of the most high God (I Ki. 19:5-5; Dan. 6:22; Mt. 4:11; Acts 10; Heb. 1:14)
5. Provide God's will (Acts 5:19-20; 10:1-6)
6. Help individuals (Mt. 18:10)
7. Sing praises and worship God (Lk. 2:13; Ps. 103:20; 148:2; Rev. 5:11)
8. Give God's laws (Acts 7:53; Heb. 2:2)
9. Bring answers to prayer (Dan. 9:21-23; 10:12-13; Acts 10)
10. Appear in dreams (Mt. 1:20-24; 2:13-19)
11. Lead sinners to salvation (Acts 10:3)
12. Guard the tree of life (Gen. 3:24)
13. Rule nations (Dan. 10:13-21; 12:1)
14. Strengthen those in trials (Mt. 4:11; Lk. 22:43)

15. Witness confession (Lk. 15:8-9)

16. Bring revelations to others (II Ki. 1:15; Dan. 8:19; 9:21-23; 10:10-20)

17. Protect the saints of God (Ps. 34:7; 91:11; Acts 12:7-11)

18. Will accompany Jesus Christ return to earth (Mt. 16:27; II Thess. 1:7-10)

19. Guard the abyss (Rev. 9:1; 20:1-3)

20. Direct the ministry of men (Acts 8:26; 27:23)

21. Will re-gather Israel (Mt. 24:31)

22. Execute judgment (Mt. 13:41-42; Acts 12:23; Rev. 8:1-9, 21; 15:1-16)

23. Wage war (Rev. 12:7-9; II Thess. 1: 7-10)

"And an angel of the Lord came up from Gilgal to Bochim, and said, I made you to go up out of Egypt, and have brought you unto the land which I sware unto your fathers; and I said, I will never break my covenant with you.

And ye shall make no league with the inhabitants of this land; ye shall throw down their altars: but ye have not obeyed my voice: why have ye done this?

Wherefore I also said, I will not drive them out from before you; but they shall be as thorns in your sides, and their gods shall be a snare unto you.

And it came to pass, when the angel of the Lord spake these words unto all the children of Israel, that the people lifted up their voice, and wept."

Judges 2:1-4

Elect Angels

Take heed that ye despise not one of these little ones; for I say unto you, That in heaven their angels do always behold the face of my Father which is in heaven.
Matthew 18:10

Chapter Five

Elect Angels

The greatest peace and comfort which can be brought to the human mind is to know that there is one who "cares for me." As the journey called life sometimes becomes treacherous and every footstep is an adventure, how exciting it can be to spend time with our spiritual Father. To be at home with Him, in the presence of the "elect" brings rewards which are not measured in earthly or financial tones.

There should be no wonder why the prodigal son (Luke 15:17) was so desirous to return to the house of his father. In a place where all those there (including the servants); are the elect and benefits are superior. It is our privilege to have a Father who cared enough to robe himself in humanity, lay down His own life and raise it up again that we may be free from the price of sin. It goes without saying how much every member of this royal family should “long” for the time to be shut in with God.

> I Timothy 5:21 “I charge thee before God, and the Lord Jesus Christ, and the elect angels, . “

These angels are chosen to be of this rank; an exalted administrative position in the Court of Heaven. These are His messengers to the elect of grace (Romans 11:5), it could even be said they are the “favorite” to serve the “favorites.” Although the mentioning of angels are throughout the Old Testament as well as the New Testaments, this is the only passage where the angels are referred to as “elect.”

With these angels to affect the souls of man, our finances and influences; we can also send them to do work which would be impossible for us otherwise. They minister to the needs of the church and are as much in demand today as they ever were. But once again, it is necessary that what we desire and seek to do is in the will of God. This once again, not to be repetitive, must be used as the gauge for all things.

Angels of Influence

In the world of spiritual warfare, each member of the army of God has a particular part to play. As with intelligence and counter-intelligence, the adversary would like for all things from the kingdom of God to be ineffective. These times can be discounted with the moments we spend in prayer. Our learning to be sensitive of the heartbeat of heaven, knowing the sound of compassion which vibrates from the throne and keeping in tune with the mind of God determines how victorious we will be.

Each warrior must understand the victory has already been predetermined. (If we will read the back of the book; the Revelation of John declares how an angel will alone bind Satan and cast him into the bottomless pit).

> Revelation 20: 1 "And I saw an angel come down from heaven, having the key of the bottomless pit and a great chain in his hand."

More than ever before, the "elect of God" need to have their influence on society. As we examine a number of examples from the Old and New Testament, we will see how the influence for the purpose of God brought victory.

In the early days of the ministry of Jesus Christ, there would have been nothing better for Satan than to see the purpose of the redeemer destroyed. Every move and detail during his life were under constant attack (does this not sound familiar for the born again believer) because of the impact He would have on mankind. When the prophesy would be fulfilled for the arrival of the King of Glory, who else but the elect angels of God to announce it.

Matthew 1:20 "behold, the angel of the Lord appeared unto him in a dream, saying, Joseph, thou son of David, fear not to take unto thee Mary thy wife: for that which is conceived in her is of the Holy Ghost."

Matthew 24:31 "And he shall send his angels with a great sound of a trumpet, and they shall gather together his elect from the four winds, from one end of heaven to the other."

Even though he could not cause Jesus Christ to fall, Satan knew the part these angels played in the spiritual world. In an attempt to cause destruction to the plan of salvation for man, our adversary thought he might also "trick" the Lord with claiming that purpose of the angel's ministry. Can we not notice once again how the "master of deception" has a knack for mixing a little truth with a lie or false pretences?

Luke 4:10 "For it is written, He shall give his angels charge over thee, to keep thee:"

(I have not at any point in this writing mentioned the fallen angels for a specific reason. Their existence is very real; their purpose to rain chaos and discord upon the Christian cannot be denied. But other than this paragraph, they will get absolutely no attention. These chapters are designed to encourage the believer with examples (both biblical and personal) and scriptures to prove not only are the angels in attendance—but can be invoked for warfare on our behalf).

Angels for the Soul

Could it not be more fitting that the body of Christ is referred to as the "elect of grace" and the angels chosen by the Almighty to do the work which deals with men are called the "elect angels." For the ransomed price that was paid for sin; the agony of shame and taste of iniquity which must have been in the bitter cup - one would have no choice to say otherwise to each of us being chosen. What an expensive price to pay for someone who does not even know you; but then again that is real love.

I am reminded of one specific session in which I went to spend time with the Lord in prayer. It had been an extremely busy day, and with all the activities of the family coming to a close—to say I was exhausted would be an understatement. I was not able to get the rest that my physical body thought it needed, but this appointment was just too important to miss.

It seemed as if I had just gone to sleep when the alarm would sound like a fire siren in my ears. Slowly dragging myself from bed to get dressed seemed nothing more than a chore of that which had to be done. All the way to this most essential meeting at the throne, I could hear myself literally fussing for the way I felt. (I understand if you have never felt this way, but I must be honest with you). Seeking ways to somehow justify returning home, and getting the rest of my sleep was all than consumed my thoughts.

Upon reaching the sanctuary and entering, another battle ensued within me. Questions of how am I going to pass these next few hours, how much water can I possibly drink or maybe I will just lay down and sleep (after all God knows I am here and He can wake me up). After a cold drink of water from the fountain and washing my hands in the restroom sink, I had no choice but to enter the auditorium.

To this day, I can not recall the doors ever shutting after my entrance. Most of the time, I would hear them and it was like a signal of the closed place in which God was with me. Today though, He spoke to me in a manner that shall forever haunt my memory. As I walked down the aisle toward the altar, with every step a statement would come from the voice of my lover—and every statement would prick my soul.

> "I did not have to die for you", "I did not have to bear the stripes on my back", "I did not have to go the the Garden in your stead", "No one made me die on Calvary for you", and last but not least "I have gone to prepare a place for you because I love you."

Needless to say, the hours flew by, there were not nearly enough of them and I dreaded to see this one end. It was here I realized I truly was "elect" when God looked from the beginning of time. He really did see me and would do all that I might have salvation. (It was in these moments I learned to be ministered by the angels and how to use them for the Kingdom.)

> Acts 10:30-32 “And Cornelius said, Four days ago I was fasting until this hour; and at the ninth hour I prayed in my house, and, behold, a man stood before me in bright clothing,
>
> And said, Cornelius, thy prayer is heard, and thine alms are had in remembrance in the sight of God.
>
> Send therefore to Joppa, and call hither Simon, whose surname is Peter; he is lodged in the house of one Simon a tanner by the sea side: who, when he cometh, shall speak unto thee.”

He was a very sincere man, one who was upright and honest in all his ways. A man, which prayed and sought the fullness of God in His life, the very attribute which was noticed. When the sincere desire for God reaches the throne, the heavens will dispatch its angels to do the work. (No where are angels of any kind the carrier of salvation (that requires a man sent from God) but these messengers can lead you and deliver the desires of your heart.

These angels get “excited” when men and women repent for their sins and desire the work of God in their life. This emotion is shown in Luke 15:10; which says “joy in the presence of the angels of God over one sinner that repenteth." Let me ask a thought provoking question at this point; if the angels get excited and they know not the power of God as we do, then how is it we can be so unemotional about our relationship with the same God?

Modern Day Society

Egotism plays a large part in this modern age, a time where men do not cry and women and children are taught to be hard and calloused. A society which advocates the hiding of emotion; for the things we are emotional about are those which matter to us. As real emotions can only come from the heart, there lies the treasures of our life.

> Matthew 6:21 "For where your treasure is, there will your heart be also."

When one becomes "emotional" and "heartfelt" about a walk with God, desires the communion with the maker above all else or refuses to hide the feelings from within about heavenly things; then the elect angels of God are there as constant companions. Who should care what others think? What does it matter - the opinions of others? Are they going to be there when I am in real need and can they make a difference?

Just as Peter needed the angel of the Lord to "deliver him out of the hand of Herod and the expectations of the Jews" (Acts 12:11); each of us will need someone higher than us to lead the way. The passion you have can and will depend on the ministering forces that travel with you in life.

> Luke 9:26 “For whosoever shall be ashamed of me and of my words, of him shall the Son of man be ashamed, when he shall come in his own glory, and in his Father’s, and of the holy angels.”
>
> Luke 12:8-9 “Also I say unto you, Whosoever shall confess me before men, him shall the Son of man also confess before the angels of God:
>
> But he that denieth me before men shall be denied before the angels of God.”

With my passion, knowing the desires of my heart and spending the time with my lover in prayer; have given me a company of ministering spirits which can be used in the will of God. From the instructions received in prayer in obedience to the will of God, I can command according to His word and will. Seeking the face of God, with His motives and purposes in mind - He will send the angels to do a swift work.

Understanding the use of personal ministering spirits is not for individual agendas. These cannot and will not be productive when one is out of the will of God. They are to be used for the victories we need and the victories of others. As we intercede for others we also may send the angels to bind, loose or deliver. Salvation and deliverance can be brought by the use of these angels who are for the elect.

> II Chronicles 32:21 "And the Lord sent an angel, which cut off all the mighty men of valour, and the leaders and captains in the camp of the king of Assyria. . ."

> Matthew 13:41 "The Son of man shall send forth his angels, and they shall gather out of his kingdom all things that offend, and them which do iniquity;"

Pray and fast! Keep the motives of the heart pure! Spend time alone with God!

By all of these, the ministering angels of God surround you; the pure heart allows one to send them with directives that give honor to God. Kingdoms and powers of darkness will be subdued—these are not fleshly fights and must be done in the spirit with spiritual elements and warriors.

And there came two angels to Sodom at even; and Lot sat in the gate of Sodom: and Lot seeing them rose up to meet them; and he bowed himself with his face toward the ground;

And he said, Behold now, my lords, turn in, I pray you, into your servant's house, and tarry all night, and wash your feet, and ye shall rise up early, and go on your ways. And they said, Nay; but we will abide in the street all night.

And he pressed upon them greatly; and they turned in unto him, and entered into his house; and he made them a feast, and did bake unleavened bread, and they did eat."

Genesis 19:1-3

Archangels

> ***"Howbeit this kind goeth not out but by prayer and fasting."***
>
> ***Matthew 17:21***

Chapter Six

Archangels

As one stands on terra firma and gazes into the heavens, he or she cannot help but wonder what must be out there. How could a world so complex and sophisticated exist that one cannot even see with the naked eyes. Understanding from the Word of God, the world which we cannot see is more real than the one we can touch and feel with human senses.

As time has passed for many generations, empires have fallen prey to their enemies and social structures have swung like a pendulum – yet the spiritual world has never given into these different attitudes or social structures. The words of the Lord in Matthew, "Heaven and earth shall pass away, but my words shall not pass away" (Matthew 24:35), can more clearly be understood. The workmanship of the operations in the "courts of heaven" has not and never will be affected by what man chooses to do or say. God has always been and always will be in control. As we have seen earlier the angels were created to worship and praise the Lord.

It is in this place, where no man can see, that a special group of angels live and are servants to the Most High. This group of very select messengers is known as the Archangels. These ministering spirits are there to protect as well as remind us of the coming of the Lord. This special group will also serve to inform each of us of the coming of the Lord and understanding end-time prophecy. Their use and the conditions for which they make themselves known must be understood in order to have a complete awareness of their existence.

Physical Kingdoms

As we look upon the world around us, many nations and kingdoms have fallen; new ones have been formed only to meet the same fate as their predecessors. Knowing we serve a God who is sovereign and all the worlds were created by Him, yet He allows us to have access as well as the blessings of these beautiful creatures of whom He made.

Colossians 1:16; “For by him were all things created, that are in heaven, and that are in earth, visible and invisible, whether they be thrones, or dominions, or principalities, or powers: all things were created by him, and for him:"

Babylon, or the Gold Kingdom, as referred to in the book of Daniel was a strong empire. Although great in strength and strongly fortified with walls around it; armies which protected it from the nations and foreign foes this great kingdom only existed from 606 B.C. to 539 B.C. The monetary system was much like the ones of modern times; money was kept in banks and temples with the interest being charged for its use. This financial system was later adopted by Greece, then the Romans and later to modern society.[3]

Nebuchadnezzar, king of Babylonia, captured Jerusalem in the year 606 B.C. (II Kings 24:1-6). It was also during this time frame in history that Daniel and the three Hebrew children went into captivity as recorded in Daniel chapter 1. The Israelites remained in captivity for seventy years and many writings of scripture were written during this period of time (Jeremiah 25, Daniel 9).[4]

Every basic reader of the Bible is familiar with the story of Abram (whose name was later changed by God to Abraham). Abram was called by God, from Ur of the Chaldees, to leave his present country and go to a place which Jehovah would reveal to him. His beginning, Ur of the Chaldees, was in Babylonia. This account for reading purposes is found in the twelfth chapter of Genesis.

In a desert region to the east and south of Babylon came another kingdom of great strength; this kingdom was known as the Media-Persian Empire. This group was led by Cyrus of Persia in 539 B.C., and was responsible for laying Babylonia to waste. During the time of a feast (Daniel 5), Cyrus sent soldiers under the walls of Babylon by the Euphrates River and killed the king of Babylonia. When the new kingdom was set up, a king by the name of Darius (from Mede) was made the ruler. It was while Darius was the ruler at Babylon where the account of Daniel and the den of lions is found in the scripture (Daniel 6).[5]

Cyrus was a great military leader, but was followed by Cambyses who was very cruel (529-522 B.C.) who took the land of Egypt and ended the rule of Pharoah. Even though Darius the Great (521-485 B.C.) was extremely powerful and very military minded; his kingdom was divided into different groups or governors. This military based kingdom ended in 331 B.C., when it fell to the Greeks.[6]

Alexander the Great took over from his father, Phillip the second of Macedonia. Educated by Aristotle, Alexander was very brilliant as well as being young (20 years of age) and strong. Amassing an army of fewer than 40,000 men, he conquered Persia and moved to conquer the Jews and the Egyptians. In 331 B.C., the final victory over Persia was given to him. This was near the area of Ninevah in Daniel 8.

As with the human nature, Alexander the Great could not be satisfied. Even though very young, after continued fighting and the conquering of India; he returned to Babylon. Alexander died at the young age of 32 years in 323 B.C. The Grecian Empire fell in 63 B.C., and another great dynasty fell by the wayside.[7]

From its small, simple setting of farmers, shepherds and various traders near the Tiber River in Italy; there arose great nations which would rule and affect major areas of history. In 63 B.C., a Roman army under the leadership of Pompey captured the city of Jerusalem. This leadership would rule from 63 B.C. until 410 A.D.

Although all these kingdoms were strong and powerful they all had one common thread which ties them together; they all fell to the element called time. No matter how great these leaders of history, past or present; they all shared the same fate. The only everlasting kingdom which will ever be is that of the King of Kings. Man is only temporal and the kingdoms which he possesses will all end up in the same fashion.

> Matthew 24:35 “Heaven and earth shall pass away, but my words shall not pass away.”

As we view the great prophets in the Old Testament, let us look at the conditions which existed and the dedication which each had toward God. Their world was very similar to the one we live in today. Although the time frame may be difficult to understand, the circumstances and social cultures were very much a mirror effect. These nations were mighty, financially sound, and socially in disarray. The voice of God was found through the writings and contact with Him.

Men such as Isaiah, Jeremiah, Daniel and Ezekiel possessed certain qualities which were more than admirable, they were necessary. Even today, in the twenty-first century, these attributes are required if each one is to hear the voice of God. These men of "old" prayed and spoke often with Jehovah. In this century, we also must speak often and clearly listen to His voice in order to be led by Him. Even the life of Moses, after leading the children of Israel from the bondage of Egypt, was required to spend time alone with God for the direction which the children were to go.

Today in modern society, we have left out the communion with God. The men of scripture each had three main characteristics. The lasting world of the unseen environment holds the key to whether we make it or fall as others have. It is imperative, no; it is an absolute necessity that each spends time alone with God to even exist in the realm which He has prepared for all who are born again believers.

Main Characteristics

First, they were men of strong convictions. Society has used words such as dysfunctional and emotionally disturbed to accept the weaknesses which exist in character. Men and women often have given way to peer pressures and the opinion of crowds, letting principles of righteousness fall by the wayside in order to be accepted. No matter how many words are used to describe sin, it still remains the same.

The prophets of old continually battled against the false of their society, those who did not have the backbone to stand for the principles of truth. If modern society and those of us who live in it do not stand strong, then we are in the same spiritual shape. God has always sought those who will stand for the truth. The prayer life which we maintain will give us the stability that is needed in a wicked and a sinful nation. The true prophets of God would not bend, bow, or keep silent where the Word of God was concerned and would not think of compromise. This generation needs strong men and women who will take the same stand for truth and what they believe. Just because it comes wrapped in the cloak of "love" and "fellowship" does not mean it is scripturally correct.

Jude warns each of us and gives explicit warning for our day against the false brethren who would lure followers away from the strong convictions needed to propagate the true gospel of salvation. Society has distorted the truth for the sake of the crowd and an easy believing system of worship which requires no stand at all. Only those who spend the necessary time alone with

God in prayer will be able to stand against the wickedness of the world and stay in contact with the Almighty.

> Philippians 2:15; "That ye may be blameless and harmless, the sons of God, without rebuke, in the midst of a crooked and perverse nation, among whom ye shine as lights in the world."

This generation can have the divine contact with God; enjoy the ministering of His angels – if we are willing to spend the time with Him in prayer. As we look at these men in old times, let us not for one moment forget that each paid the price of time alone with Jehovah. The only force which can stabilize us comes from the world which cannot be seen with natural eyes and understood with human thinking. It was their prayer that gave them the strong convictions, constant contact with one more powerful than the physical.

Secondly, they were men of strong commitment. Although God is sovereign, He still uses men to do the work in this world. Our spiritual battles are won when God is satisfied with the work that is being accomplished. We can only complete the work for Him if we spend the necessary time in prayer to know the perfect will of God in our life.

When we set our own goals and have forgotten our true purpose, then our lives are not complete and failure will follow. In one of the few commands which the Lord Jesus Christ gave to each of us, “But seek ye first the kingdom of God, and his righteousness; and all these things shall be added unto you.” (Matthew 6:33). When we have a healthy and fruitful prayer life, then we will know the will and mind of God for each situation which arises.

It was the determined dedication to the Word and work of God which made Jeremiah a champion. His labor was in full harmony and peace with God in the face of what most would judge as unfair and consider a failure. He had no great campaign revival, no popular respect, no physical respite, and was continually persecuted; but still he remained faithful to the call of God without ever compromising what was right. It was the sheer determination to carry out the will of God that made him one of the greatest prophets in the Old Testament.

Today, peer pressure, public opinion, and personal kingdom goals can cause the direction which many take to be far from the direction of God. The Lord is not looking for those with a large ego or personal desire, but men and women who are determined to know the will of God and work to satisfy Him alone. The cry of Joshua has been hung upon many a wall in the living room, placed perfectly upon the door to the home or in the entrance to the sanctuary, but never upon the heart of our soul. Joshua 24:15, ". . . as for me and my house, we will serve the Lord."

Only when we pray and seek the face of God will we be able to stand in the face of adversity and not be moved. Daniel in the den of lions is a perfect example of those who stand true to God. How can we have the visitation of the most beautiful creatures of heaven, if we do not pay the price? How can one have the use of the angelic hosts with a mind and attitude that continually is upon things of this world?

Thirdly, they were men of extreme commitment and challenge. Whether in the mind or on the battlefield of life, victories are won when total commitment is made against the enemy. The world today taunts the church as well as all who dare to be different. If someone spends time in prayer, they are considered "weird" or those who show emotion for the cause of Christ are considered "radical" and shunned. The atheists, agnostics and the infidels spend an excessive amount of time to promote their causes of false hopes; God is looking for men and women who will offer to Him the extreme commitment and have the provisions of heaven at their disposal.

Half-hearted efforts based upon the visual results will never accomplish the will of God. The Lord seeks men and women who like the prophets of old, will never waver or falter but will give themselves even unto death.

Having divine visitations from the angelic host of heaven will require a challenge to each and every human being. A spiritually hungry individual who is willing to spend the time with God, no matter what anyone says, will be assured of such a visit. Service and honesty from the heart is only seen and will only be known by God.

The Archangels

The word archangel occurs several times in the bible. In the celestial hierarchy; it is a spiritual being next in rank above an angel.[8] The word archangel occurs several times in the Bible. In the New Testament the voice of an archangel and the sounding of the trumpet of God will signal the coming of Christ for his people. The archangel, at the immediate notice from God, will sound the welcome "invitation" which the Church has been longing to hear. All those who are the Bride of Christ, those purchased by His blood will be called to the Marriage Supper of the Lamb.

> I Thessalonians 4: 16; "For the Lord himself shall descend from heaven with a shout, with the voice of the archangel, and with the trump of God: and the dead in Christ shall rise first:"
>
> I Thessalonians 4:17; "Then we which are alive and remain shall be caught up together with them in the

clouds, to meet the Lord in the air: and so shall we ever be with the Lord."

Those who have spent time in prayer and dedication to Him will be called up to the reward of the faithful. All the consecrated efforts put forth will be worth every amount of energy spent. Let each of us remain constant in our efforts to the Kingdom of God and seek His will and desire for our personal lives.

The two most popular archangels are Michael and Gabriel. Let us notice the scriptures where each are spoken of and notice the representation of the authority which both have been given. Also, let us notice the life of the person to whom they are sent. It is of great importance that we understand the type of life and the commitment that each had. As we study this particular section, the archangels, if we are to have access to their ministry then our lifestyle must be comparable in nature to theirs.

Convictions of Daniel

Daniel was a man of strong convictions, one of the young Hebrews carried into the Babylonian captivity by King Nebuchadnezzar when he conquered Judah around 605 B.C. Daniel and the other Hebrews were confronted with foreign ideas and customs, but Daniel took a stand for what he knew was right. Because of his sterling character, God brought him into favor with the king of Babylon, who elevated him to an important governmental position.

Daniel proved valuable to the Babylonians by interpreting visions and dreams and by his wise administration of government offices. Yet Daniel did not get so involved in his work that he neglected his relationship with God. His devotion was soon known by many people, even to those who sought his destruction.

Daniel's godly life and executive position, however, stirred others to envy, and his enemies soon conspired against him. They tried to catch him in wrongdoing, but found nothing against him. They then set a trap for Daniel, who refused to change his daily devotions to God.

> Daniel 6:4; "Then the presidents and princes sought to find occasion against Daniel concerning the kingdom; but they could find none occasion nor fault; forasmuch as he was faithful, neither was there any error or fault found in him."

Often it may seem we are wasting time or the times we pause for daily devotionals to God are only holding us up from doing other items of importance. But never do we spend time in prayer or reading of the scriptures which results in a waste. God will honor our consistency and dedication to him. Each one desires, and we often look at Daniel with a sense of fascination because of what he went through and accomplished. It is necessary for us to understand the dedications he made to Jehovah. Every modern day Christian may escape the den of lions, but other situations will arise in our lives and we can have the same ministering angel as Daniel – if and when – we live with the same amount of consistency. As a result, he was cast to the lions, but the Lord honored Daniel's belief in Him, and rescued him. The same can be said today; the Lord has not changed nor lost His power due to time and age.

Daniel's commitment to God was so well known that Ezekiel, his contemporary, mentioned him three times as an example of righteousness and wisdom. Daniel's habits are a good pattern for those who aspire to a closer walk with God. It is inspiring to study a life that the devil could not fault or touch; a life that God blessed greatly.

There are those in Christendom who desire to have their names and reputation enhanced by the populous of society. It is not that important and will amount to nothing if their popularity does not exist for the right purpose. Not only did Ezekiel know of Daniel's reputation, the devil also knew it and was determined to destroy him. If we are known in the courts of heaven and the halls of hell, that alone should be our goal.

> Ezekiel 14:14; "Though these three men, Noah, Daniel, and Job, were in it, they should deliver but

their own souls by their righteousness, saith the Lord God."

Ezekiel 14:20; "Though Noah, Daniel, and Job, were in it, as I live, saith the Lord God, they shall deliver neither son nor daughter; they shall but deliver their own souls by their righteousness."

Ezekiel 28:3; "Behold, thou art wiser than Daniel; there is no secret that they can hide from thee:"

Because of his commitment, dedication and habits of seeking the face of God, his prayers were answered. During the time of prayer and fasting and his petition to God, the archangel of the Lord was dispatched to assist in giving the victory.

Daniel 8:16; "and said, Gabriel, make this man to understand the vision"

Daniel 10:13; "but, lo, Michael, one of the chief princes, came to help me; and I remained there with the kings of Persia."

Leadership of Moses

There are many men and women in churches today who desire to be in a leadership position. Just as God used the crucible of circumstances to affect His will throughout the lives of Daniel, Moses and Joseph, we must also let this same changing cycle take place in our lives. There is more to leadership than just the position of an exalted state. Leaders and leadership positions have great value in the kingdom of God; they must also be given because of an equal amount of dedication and seasoning.

When God chose Moses to lead Israel out of Egyptian bondage, he answered the call with faith and obedience. In leaving the riches of Pharaoh's palace for his people, Moses demonstrated his faith in God that his people were destined for greater riches. Having been raised in Pharaoh's house, he was trained in all the knowledge and wisdom of this advanced civilization. However, being motivated by influences in his early life through the design of God, Moses forsook his claim to royalty and forsook the life of leisure, fame, and riches.

Time in faithful service to God will lead anyone who desires to a place of leadership for the Kingdom. Just as the Lord was faithful to Moses, we must understand that Moses was faithful to the Lord. As we will notice in the scripture, Moses was valuable enough to God that the archangel Michael would wrestle for the body of this leader.

In modern society, there is a cry from heaven for those who are more interested in being fought over for their spiritual value than fighting for an economic value. Men today can be bought and sold for pennies; where as heaven's value is much more than all the money this world has to offer.

In the same way that godly leadership was needed for the people of Israel, it is needed in our world today. There is always a need for Christian leaders who will sacrifice their time and talents and give themselves wholly to God. The desire and need for human approval can only lead to very short-lived satisfaction considering that God's approval leads to an eternity of rewards. God empowers such individuals not only for the benefit of the church but also for the needs of societies and governments as well.

True Christian leaders manifest a servant's heart. They willingly lay self-glorification and pride on the altar of prayer and sacrifice. Godly leaders, like shepherds, go before the people, providing appropriate direction, leadership and guidance.

Having been chosen by God, and answering the call; Moses had the divine protection of God. Each of us today can answer the call with our prayer and faithfulness to God alone. Since his loyalty and prayer to God was the basic foundation to his life while living, at his death the Lord dispatched the archangel at the time of his death.

> Jude 9; "Yet Michael the archangel, when contending with the devil he disputed about the body of Moses,

durst not bring against him a railing accusation, but said, The Lord rebuke thee."

Power and Authority

As we have noticed a number of similarities in the lives of Daniel and Moses, these too can be credited to our individual lives. In study of the power and responsibility of the archangel, if we will pray and seek time with God, the responses to other servants will be provided for us.

When compared to Daniel chapter ten; however, we see that Michael is evidently only one of the archangels (Daniel 10:13). Furthermore, Michael appears to be in charge of the angels with regard to the nation of Israel.

> Daniel 10:21; "But I will shew thee that which is noted in the scripture of truth: and there is none that holdeth with me in these things, but Michael your prince."

> Daniel 12:1; "And at that time shall Michael stand up, the great prince which standeth for the children of thy people: and there shall be a time of trouble, such as never was since there was a nation even to that same

> time: and at that time thy people shall be delivered, every one that shall be found written in the book."

It is possible that Gabriel, a notable angel of the Bible, may also be an archangel. While the Scriptures do not specifically name any archangels other than Michael, Gabriel has a prominent place among the named angels. Gabriel made the significant announcement regarding the birth of John the Baptist and also of the Messiah Himself.

> Luke 1:11; "And there appeared unto him an angel of the Lord standing on the right side of the altar of incense."

> Luke 1:26; "And in the sixth month the angel Gabriel was sent from God unto a city of Galilee, named Nazareth,"

Gabriel was also sent by God to deliver to Daniel the understanding of the dream which the king had. It also would seem he was possibly God's foremost spokesman from the realm of the angelic host. Gabriel, Michael and Lucifer (Satan) are the only three angels identified by name in the Word of God.

As we have viewed this special group of ministering spirits, let us evaluate our life; let each of us look at the purpose for which we live and how our goals are set in relationship to the kingdom of God. If we will pray and seek the leadership of heaven, then those ministering spirits will also direct, instruct and lead us.

I will not say emphatically that this author has had a visitation from an archangel, but the experience which would fit in line with these examples of scripture took place a number of years ago. I was ministering in a place which was bound by a particular religious dominion and the stronghold seemed to be unbreakable. After much prayer and seeking the will of God on how to set men free from this oppression, the Lord spoke to me concerning a season of fasting.

After a few weeks of fasting and prayer, early one morning I saw the representative of this particular system walk through the entrance of the church where I was praying. As this "spirit" entered the foyer, he made his way toward the sanctuary where I was in prayer.

When he reached the entrance to the sanctuary, there seemed to be a glass wall that stopped him. After trying for a number of times to get through the invisible wall of glass, he retreated and in a spirit of authority spoke two words which I will always remember. After backing away and a little closer to the entrance he said, "YOU WIN!" and left for good.

After that a number of families came to know the Lord and experience the joy of salvation which all are meant to have. The oppression from the adversary had been broken; but only after fasting and prayer.

"So he drove out the man; and he placed at the east of the garden of Eden Cherubims, and a flaming sword which turned every way, to keep the way of the tree of life."

Genesis 3:24

"The Lord reigneth; let the people tremble: he sitteth between the cherubims; let the earth be moved."

Psalms 99:1

Cherubims

"(For the weapons of our warfare are not carnal, but mighty through God to the pulling down of strong holds;)"

II Corinthians 10:4

Chapter Seven

Cherubims

Cherub, Cherubim, appears in the Hebrew only about sixty times in the Old Testament and is from the Hebrew *"kerubim,"* meaning to "grasp or that which grasps, or holds.[9]

Cheroubim are regarded by some as the ideal representatives of redeemed animate creation. In the tabernacle and Temple they were represented by the two golden figures of two-winged living creatures. They were all of one piece with the golden lid of the Ark of the Covenant in the Holy of Holies signifying that the prospect of redeemed and glorified creatures was bound up with the sacrifice of Christ.

This in itself would indicate that they represent redeemed human beings in union with Christ, a union seen, figuratively, proceeding out of the mercy seat. Their faces were towards this mercy seat, suggesting a consciousness of the means whereby union with Christ has been produced. In the NT the word is found in Heb. 9:5, where the reference is to the ark in the tabernacle, and the thought is suggested of those who minister to the manifestation of the glory of God.

> ceroubivm cheároáubim, kher-oo-beem´; plur. of Heb. or. "cherubim" (i.e. cherubs or kerubim):—cherubims.

It would seem not to be an accident that the first angelic references in the scripture would be these beautiful creations from God. The cherubims are the protectors of God's holiness and these angels "hold or grasp" that which rightfully belongs to the Almighty. Because of their disobedience (Adam and Eve) to God and the separation which sin leaves in our lives, their expulsion from the Garden of Eden was necessary. In order to protect what was holy and to assure it would stay that way, the angel was posted as a guard to the Tree of Knowledge of good and evil (Genesis 3:24). The cheribums are related to the protection of the holiness of God in relation to sin.

Failure of Man

After their expulsion from the Garden of Eden, humanity needed the redemption from the "wages of sin." The separation caused by sin now caused a wide void between man and a holy God. The beautiful communion which took place each evening (Genesis 3:8) as the Spirit of God would walk through the Garden of Eden for a time of fellowship with Adam and Eve.

Man was, has been, and always will be a free-will agent of his own destiny. The decision Adam and Eve made were choices on their own volition and each man and woman will make theirs just the same. Satan was not content to enjoy his exalted place as an angel. It was his desire to be like God that pushed him over the boundary of this existence in Heaven's Courts and was the reason for the fall which now consumes every person born of woman.

Lucifer, that archangel, whose name has been defined as meaning "light-bringer" and "brightness," enjoyed one of the most coveted places as one of God's creations. As "son of the morning," he was at the zenith of his glory. When the rebellion consumed him, the process began which would eventually spiral him downward to the nadir of his existence and eventually to the lake of fire.

The rebellion of Lucifer was now placed within the heart of the first two humans, a beauty of the craftsmanship of the Almighty God. Even though it was a very deceptive way to introduce it, nevertheless, Satan had found others to enjoy his delightful conspiracy. His introduction was one of half-truth in a question which made the sin seem to be beneficial.

We find in the approach which the serpent used, the core of all deception used today. The first correspondence with Eve was to trick her through her appetite (lust of the flesh), through the appearance of the fruit (lust of the eyes), and through her ambition to attain knowledge which had been forbidden to her to be like God (pride of life). Adam soon followed her persuasion without being tempted by the serpent. His was an inward temptation and was much more deliberate and openly rebellious than that of his wife.

> I John 3:4 "Whosoever committeth sin transgresseth also the law: for sin is the transgression of the law."

> I John 2:16 "For all that is in the world, the lust of the flesh, and the lust of the eyes, and the pride of life, is not of the Father,"

Let us not get caught up in the "Fall of Man" and forget the beautiful picture which has been painted for us by the hand of God. No, this tree in the Garden was not to be touched and the consequences must be paid for the sin which the inhabitants committed. As we examine further we can also see the mercy which was showed by placing the angel with a flaming sword to guard it. Since it would have meant complete death to all, the angel actually served as a protector and allowed God to redeem them. This tree is only mentioned twice in the scriptures. The first time is east of Eden (Genesis 2:17) and the next time will be for the redeemed saints (Revelation 2:7).

Separated From God

Since we are looking at how to use these ministering spirits in our walk with God, it would be helpful to have a good understanding of what not to become involved in. Since the successful walk with God depends upon our constant communication with Him, our openness to His will, and the state of affairs in our heart; knowing what He abhors will do nothing but add strength to each life.

Just as in the Garden of Eden, sin separated mankind from God. Even though He loved Adam and Eve, the sin (rebellion) which was now present caused a large void with a holy and righteous Creator. When we understand just what rebellion is and consists of, then we are able to avoid it entirely. (We will not dwell long on this part of the subject, but as one man once said, “an ounce of prevention is better than a pound of cure.”)

We know that sin brings forth death (James 1:15) and that sin can be avoided. Mankind does not have to commit sin. Here one can find another philosophy which exists in our world and is another deception from the "belly of the deceiver." We cannot continually live in sin and be the temple of the living God (I John 3:8).

1. Sin is an overstepping of the divine Law of God. The transgression of God's will in our life. This nature (Psalms 51:5; Luke 15:29) is born in each of us at birth and one could say "it is part of the package" from which we must be delivered from. We usurp the authority of God in our life and manifest a spirit of insubordination. We become used by a disqualified (Satan) authority and participate in wrong instead of right.

2. Sin is an inherently wrong act that is forbidden by God. It is iniquity, a lawless nature and act toward those given to us by the Lord. It is the condition of not being right either by God's standards or with your relationship, according to those things which man knows to be correct or right by the conscience (Romans 9:14). It is the wrong, injury or misdeed and denotes wickedness (Romans 1:29; I Corinthians 5:8).

3. Sin is the departure or error from that which is right. The going in the wrong direction from the desires of God which have been forbidden by His Word (Romans 3:23). When we ally ourselves with the forces of the adversary and the attitudes

which were brought from the beginning, we are courting destruction. Sin causes us to move away from that which is right and moral; to move in the direction of evil and darkness.

4. When we fail to meet the divine standard, to fall short of our best, and to be chained to the ugly; we allow ourselves to be a hedonist. When we miss the mark and become spiritually delinquent and criminal, a non-law-abiding person we have become ensnared by sin. The attitude of our personal desires no matter what the consequences and the washing away of the inward man – then the spirit of disobedience has taken control of our life.

5. Sin is the intrusion of self-will into the arena of God's Divine authority (Ephesians 2:1). When we begin to trespass this territory and exercise self-will over that of God's Word, it is putting ourselves in the same position of rule. The spirit of deception will cause us to seek "my" will more than "His" will in everything which I pursue. The spirit of sin is the embryo of an apostate and a blasphemer. Therefore, with this attitude and feeling it is impossible to please God.

6. Sin is when the lawless nature and spiritual order has become lost (I Timothy 1:9). Sin causes the

heart to become deceived and distorts the vision from God in our lives and heart, creating mass confusion as well as distrust. Satan did this with the tree in the Garden of Eden.

7. Sin causes a spirit of unbelief. We consummate an attitude of insult to divine truths (St. John 16:9). We doubt the very nature of the Bible and those promises (blessing and curses) which are held within its pages. When doubt has been planted and the lack of trust in the scriptures is rampant in our spirit, we bind the very purpose of the trip to Calvary by Jesus Christ.[10]

Redemption with Mercy

Since sin had now separated man from the maker, God began to "work" and remove that which became the void for a once beautiful relationship. As the beautiful plan would unfold, it was necessary that God reveal to all humanity that His Holiness was very important and a necessity which could not ever be overlooked. The sinful nature of humanity would most definitely have grace and mercy extended to them, but the purity must be understood if such a relationship was to ever exist again.

What started out with about seventy people who would seek refuge from a drought when Joseph was sold into slavery by his brothers; now had become a nation of about three million people. After approximately four hundred and thirty years of captivity, the children of Jehovah would finally be set free. As Moses would lead the Children of Israel through the Red Sea and into the wilderness, the plan and provisions of God would take place for all.

Once they had been delivered from Egypt, Moses would make a trip to Mount Sinai and receive the instructions of God for all those of the Dispensation of the Law. It was there that Jehovah would give the law of proper worship and obedience which would become knows as the Ten Commandments.

Instructions for the Tabernacle would be very specific. In fact, all directions and instructions from God are always specific. When it comes to worship, praise, repentance and living; God does not vary one small fraction from His Word. As we take a look at three particular aspects of the Tabernacle, we also see the importance of holiness with God.

1. <u>We see a figure</u>. A figure is an outline, or a sketch of a particular object. As we study and look closely to that all which the Lord showed to Moses, we will notice the earthly Tabernacle is a "figure" of the Heavenly Tabernacle. Further reading can be done in Hebrews 9:8-9, 23-24. If

the holiness of God was and is an important part of the earthly, it most certainly will be essential for the Heavenly Tabernacle.

2. We see a shadow. A shadow is a reflection from another light. When the light of God is shining, its image is a reflection upon the earthly. In the Tabernacle on the earth, the reflection most assuredly was a reflection of that from the heavens. We can find this in Hebrews 10:1.

3. We see a pattern. A pattern is an example of the things which are in heaven. The tabernacle plan given to Moses was an example of the heavenly tabernacle. Read Hebrews 8:5; I Corinthians 10:11; Luke 24:44 for additional scriptures. As we look at the tabernacle, notice the importance of the Cherubims (protectors of God's holiness).

As the children of Israel would awaken every morning, the first thing they would see from their tent door was a large walled structure known as the tabernacle. It was inside this structure where the presence of Jehovah would dwell and the atonement for the sins of those who sacrificed would be rolled ahead for another year. In the directions from Jehovah on the mount, certain materials and decorations were to be used; this would reflect the type of environment and presence of God in their lives.

The Tabernacle

> Exodus 25:8; “And let them make me a sanctuary; that I may dwell among them.

> Ex 25:9; According to all that I shew thee, after the pattern of the tabernacle, and the pattern of all the instruments thereof, even so shall ye make it.”

Inside this rectangular structure was the Shechinah of Jehovah. It was here that God would meet with the Priesthood and accept the sins of the people. This place had to be a reflection according to the tabernacle in the heavens in order to serve its purpose. As we look at only those aspects which pertain to this particular subject, notice how important each one is. The plan given to Moses by Jehovah was a once and for all plan. There will never be any additions or addendums to this plan, God gave it specifically and it will always be the same. The words of God are specific and never need to be changed.

Every detail had a specific purpose, prophetic and redemptive significance. Since God was the master architect, and every aspect which reflected His character, holiness, detail of redemption and validity of the unchanging Word. We will not examine the structure nor the furnishings in great detail, only examine those which pertain to this reading; but these which we review will give us an insight to the importance things hold in our relationship with God.

The Mercy Seat

Exodus 25:18-20 "And thou shalt make two cherubims of gold, of beaten work shalt thou make them, in the two ends of the mercy seat.

And make one cherub on the one end, and the other cherub on the other end: even of the mercy seat shall ye make the cherubims on the two ends thereof.

And the cherubims shall stretch forth their wings on high, covering the mercy seat with their wings, and their faces shall look one to another; toward the mercy seat shall the faces of the cherubims be."

The first time we saw the cherubim, these beautiful creatures were standing guard in the Garden of Eden to assure that a sin-infested man would not partake of the tree. Now on the second occasion, we see the angel in the very house of worship for His people. The figure of "His holiness against sin" now would be located on the mercy seat.

The Ark was a chest or "box" of incorruptible wood, covered with pure gold, both inside and out (Exodus 25:10-16). There were two handles by which the Ark could be carried. The Mercy Seat was the "lid" and made of solid gold with touching wings. Between the cherubim's shone the Shechinah fire of God's presence. Inside this chest contained the tables of stone (Ten Commandments), a golden pot of manna, and Aaron's rod that budded.

Mercy seat in Hebrew literally means "a blood covering." One thing the Mercy Seat covered was the Ten Commandments, the Law which calls heaven and earth to record against every soul, for every soul is guilty of breaking some part of God's Law. The sins of Israel were there, and the eyes of God were looking down upon them. The Mercy Seat shows the "mercy" of God, the fire will consume the sacrifice of our wrongs as we look upon them if we will ask.

Ark of the Covenant

Just as God would dwell with the people in the tabernacle, His spirit was shown in the many pieces of furniture throughout time. The cherubim were more than clouds or statues are plain from the description Ezekiel gives us in Ezekiel 10:1-22; which shows that they are the "living creatures" of the first chapter. They were winged creatures with features both animal and human.

Each had four faces; of a man, a lion on the right side; of an ox on the left side; also of an eagle.

It has been said that the typology of these "living creature" are representatives of character. These four faces are thought to be qualities which belong to God's redeemed people. Let us look in passing at what each one would represent. Not only do we find the symbols of man and animal, each would face in four different directions. These directions are symbolical of the four-corners of the earth or all four corners of the globe. Let it also be noted that each had wings, this is symbolical of the flying or the swiftness by their obedience which each one reacts.

1. The man – would represent the intelligence and wisdom. Truly when we are in contact with God and study the Word, wisdom does become a basic part of our life.

2. The ox – this would represent the strength. The Bible most assuredly gives each born again believer the strength each needs. One of the greatest advantages of a Christian is the strength to go through situations in life.

3. The lion – this represents the kingly authority. It is common knowledge that the lion is the king of all beasts. This four-footed animal is known for the fierceness which he represents;

as a child of God, there should be great tenacity and determination in living a life of victory.

4. <u>The eagle</u> – this would represent the swiftness and far-sightedness that this beautiful bird displays. The eagle can with one smooth stroke of its powerful wings fly about one-half mile. The eagle is not intimidated by the strong winds and storms, in fact, just the opposite is true; it is in the strongest of storms the eagle can be most effective. A Christian can show their true colors often in extremely stressful times.

The Ark of the Covenant, the symbol of the Presence of God was very sacred to the Israelites. Oftentimes they would enter into battle with the Ark of the Covenant; it showed the enemy that the God they served was with them. This presence is manifested today by the presence of the Holy Spirit in our lives.

The two cherubim placed by Solomon in the holy of holies were made of olive wood and overlaid with gold. We can notice the importance in these “living creatures” by scriptural locations where the presence of God would dwell.

I Kings 8: 6,7; “And the priests brought in the ark of the covenant of the Lord unto his place, into the oracle of the house, to the most holy place, even under the wings of the cherubims.

For the cherubims spread forth their two wings over the place of the ark, and the cherubims covered the ark and the staves thereof above."

II Chronicles 5:7,8; "And the priests brought in the ark of the covenant of the Lord unto his place, to the oracle of the house, into the most holy place, even under the wings of the cherubims:

For the cherubims spread forth their wings over the place of the ark, and the cherubims covered the ark and the staves thereof above."

Hebrews 9:5; "And over it the cherubims of glory shadowing the mercyseat; of which we cannot now speak particularly."

Walls and Curtains

One would enter on the east gate, actually four posts which represented the four Gospels (Matthew, Mark, Luke and John) which tell of the life of In order for one to understand exactly about the structure of the tabernacle, let us very briefly look at the outlay in terms of the way it was designed. When one thinks of walls and curtains, we most commonly imagine that of a home;

yet there was no structure before or since that had the design of this “home of the glory of God?”

This rectangular shape was centered inside the camp of Israel. The east side and the west side were seventy-five feet wide, the north and south sides were one hundred fifty feet long. Upon entrance one would see the Outer Court which consisted of the Brazen Altar and Brazen Laver. The Inner Court was the place where only the Priesthood could go to meet with Jehovah.

In the Inner Court were the Table of Shewbread, Candlesticks and the Altar of Incense. After passing through a veil, the Priest would enter into the Holy of Holies, it was there the Ark of the Covenant and the Mercy Seat was kept.

There were four coverings which were spread over the framework. The outer covering was of badger skin, then the ram’s skin dyed red, a third of white goat’s hair, and the fourth of fine twine linen. We will not at this time discuss any of the coverings except the fourth of fine twine linen. There would be absolutely no way in this size of study since the Tabernacle alone could and would consume many volumes.

> Exodus 26:1 “Moreover thou shalt make the tabernacle with ten curtains of fine twined linen, and blue, and purple, and scarlet: with cherubims of cunning work shalt thou make them.”

There were ten of these fine twined linen curtains. They were placed under the goats' hair curtains and formed the ceiling of the Tabernacle. They were dropped over the outside of the boards, leaving the golden boards for the walls. They were shorter than the other curtains, not being allowed to touch the ground. This typology shows us that even though Jesus Christ came to the earth; His purity was never contaminated by the world where He came to live. Just as Hebrews 7:26 tells us "He was holy, harmless, undefiled, seperated from sinners."

Cherubim were embroidered on the white linen in blue, purple and scarlet. Notice the following scriptures which the outspread wings of the cherubim overhead will give credence to.

> Psalms 61:4 "I will abide in thy tabernacle for ever: I will trust in the cover of thy wings. Selah."

> Psalms 63:7 "Because thou hast been my help, therefore in the shadow of thy wings will I rejoice."

> Psalms 91:4 "He shall cover thee with his feathers, and under his wings shalt thou trust: his truth shall be thy shield and buckler."

Psalms 36:7 “How excellent is thy lovingkindness, O God! therefore the children of men put their trust under the shadow of thy wings.”

This place may not have been the most beautiful home, but it was where Jehovah met with His people. Inside this very “crude” structure was the Holy One of Israel and He met with those who desired Him.

The Laver

Although one would think it well enough that every place they looked, the cherubim was there; and that should be enough to remind us of the holiness which these living creatures represented. As we have seen from the Garden of Eden to the Tree of Life in Revelation, as well as the complete structure shown to Moses on the Mount – the cherubim was a very important statement in light of redemption and grace.

When Solomon built the temple to worship the God of Israel, no expense or beauty was spared. These celestial creatures played a very important part in the tabernacle and rightly so; they were protectors of God for the people dedicated to Him.

We find in the following verse, Solomon even had the cherubim on the laver. The laver was more than just a bowl of water. The laver is symbolical of washing;

representing the burial of Christ. Christ's burial is our cleansing; the burial in water as proof of the cleansing. When we are "buried" with Him in baptism, we can rise to newness of life.

> I Kings 7: 29 "And on the borders that were between the ledges were lions, oxen, and cherubims: and upon the ledges there was a base above: and beneath the lions and oxen were certain additions made of thin work."

> I Kings 7:36 "For on the plates of the ledges thereof, and on the borders thereof, he graved cherubims, lions, and palm trees, according to the proportion of every one, and additions round about."

Personal Application

As we look at the tabernacle, it is easy to become excited about the plan, provisions by Jehovah and what it means to Christians today. A plan so beautifully orchestrated and designed that it would never need to be changed or reworked. But, just as it was symbolical – there was also a part which was very real.

One constant which was there and needs to be in our life today is prayer. The Priest would attach a rope to their feet and if there was sin in their life, they would then be struck dead by God and would have to be dragged out. Their dedication and holiness was very important, it was life or death.

Actually, even today – holiness is a life and death situation. The power which is in prayer is limitless because God is limitless. He is the all powerful one, and when a man or woman prays he is contacting the God who brought the Children of Israel through the wilderness. The only thing which God cannot do is commit sin. Through the avenue of prayer, God places His total resources within reach of the believer.

If we will dedicate ourselves to Him alone, He alone will deliver each place which life leads us. The Priest was required to stay holy; the cherubim were symbolical of that condition. We may not be immediately struck down, but death is assured if we do not keep our lives holy. His holiness demands that our sin and transgressions be judged.

"Above it stood the seraphims: each one had six wings; with twain he covered his face, and with twain he covered his feet, and with twain he did fly."

Isaiah 6:2

"Then flew one of the seraphims unto me, having a live coal in his hand, which he had taken with the tongs from off the altar:

And he laid it upon my mouth, and said, Lo, this hath touched thy lips; and thine iniquity is taken away, and thy sin purged."

Isaiah 6: 6-7

Seraphims

"Praying always with all prayer and supplication in the Spirit, and watching thereunto with all perseverance and supplication for all saints;"

Ephesians 6:18

Chapter Eight

Seraphims

The Bible does not mention the seraphim very much. The only place where these living creatures are mentioned can be found in Isaiah chapter 6. They are thought to be comparable to the cherubim in Ezekiel and Revelation.

Seraphim, (burning, glowing),[11] an order of celestial beings; whom Isaiah beheld in vision standing above Jehovah as he sat upon his throne. (Isaiah 6:2). They are described as having each of them three pairs of wings, with one of which they covered their faces (a token of humility); with the second they covered their feet (a token of respect); while with the third they flew.

SERAPHIMS- from the Hebrew "seraphim."

The only reference given to these beautiful creatures found in the scriptures are in these specific passages. It is thought that their service to God is that of one who protects the glory of God against sinful man. They are often compared to the four living creatures of Ezekiel and the book of Revelation.

> Ezekiel 1:6-11; “And every one had four faces, and every one had four wings.
>
> And their feet were straight feet; and the sole of their feet was like the sole of a calf's foot: and they sparkled like the colour of burnished brass.
>
> And they had the hands of a man under their wings on their four sides; and they four had their faces and their wings.
>
> Their wings were joined one to another; they turned not when they went; they went every one straight forward.
>
> As for the likeness of their faces, they four had the face of a man, and the face of a lion, on the right side: and they four had the face of an ox on the left side; they four also had the face of an eagle.
>
> Thus were their faces: and their wings were stretched upward; two wings of every one were

joined one to another, and two covered their bodies."

Revelation 4:6-8; And before the throne there was a sea of glass like unto crystal: and in the midst of the throne, and round about the throne, were four beasts full of eyes before and behind.

And the first beast was like a lion, and the second beast like a calf, and the third beast had a face as a man, and the fourth beast was like a flying eagle.

And the four beasts had each of them six wings about him; and they were full of eyes within: and they rest not day and night, saying, Holy, holy, holy, Lord God Almighty, which was, and is, and is to come."

It can also be noted that in the Old Testament, the same word is used to describe the serpent in the wilderness (Numbers 21:6-8). These ministering angels were seen by the Prophet Isaiah as having hands, faces and voices of men. We find that the wings covered their faces and feet.

These beautiful creatures took an unusual posture, one which symbolizes the respect and awe of Almighty God. Their wings are a testament of the speed which each possessed.

Time of Isaiah

Since there is so little written in the Bible about the seraphim, one of the best ways to understand these angels would be to take into account the condition of Israel. As one who was often called the great evangelical prophet since he often spoke of salvation from Jehovah, Isaiah was a citizen of Jerusalem. It is believed that he was a member of the upper echelon of the city.

A little more than two hundred years before him, the Kingdom had been divided into the Northern and Southern Kingdom. Israel was deep in idolatry when Isaiah's prophetic ministry began. The kings were wicked, and suffered through civil wars and conflicts with the heathen nations around it.

All was bleak around him, a nation which was filled with idolatry and a king who had absolutely no respect for the God of Israel. Uzziah was king of Judah when Isaiah began his prophetic ministry. He was a good king, and had favor with Isaiah. Under his reign (Uzziah), the kingdom became proud and intruded into the office of the priest. As a punishment for his sin, he was smitten with leprosy until the day he died (II Chronicles 26:16-23).

When Uzziah died, Isaiah became focused on someone other than the king to whom he served. It was at this time, a change of leadership in the Kingdom –

which a startling revelation came to the prophet of God. His eyes were taken away from where he lived and placed upon the God he served.

A View of His Glory

> Isaiah 6:1 "In the year that king Uzziah died I saw also the Lord sitting upon a throne, high and lifted up, and his train filled the
> temple."

With his eyes away from the surrounding circumstances, alone in the Temple of the Lord; there Isaiah saw the one to whom he really served. It was only after the death of Uzziah, the look to a higher power, and an experience that would change him forever.

Having been accustomed to all the glory, formality, royalty, and crowns; it must have seemed a little strange the last few years of Uzziah's life. The prophet was familiar with the throne room in the palace and when the king became ill with the leprosy, his seat of high honor was most likely left vacant. When entering the throne room – one can almost imagine the "vacant" feeling which no doubt consumed his thoughts.

After the death of his friend, Isaiah was now in a lonely position; the loss of a loved one or friend can often leave life seeming a little vacant. It was at this time that he would enter the temple and receive a revelation of unforgettable impact. Many times in our lives, there are situations that arise which leave us searching for answers. These instances can have a lasting impact upon anyone; we can make them useful and receive the blessings or give into the loss and allow it to take control of our thoughts.

Upon entering the temple, a vision of real glory comes before the eyes of one who was acquainted with those who wear royal robes and crowns. Only this time, the apparel was worn by one whose glory and honor had never been seen by these eyes. The magnitude of glory had never been witnessed before by any human being.

The throne which he saw was high and lifted up; it was in a place of distinct honor and power. The glory and righteousness of this one was one which was beyond all imagination and mental conception. Having lived and served a king who was not righteous, Isaiah was not too familiar with the wearer of a crown of such prestige. The crown and glory train which this vision showed was somewhat new to even this prophet.

Only a vision such as this can change men. All humanity is accustomed to the natural beauty and those who are in positions of prestige; those who demand honor to get it. This royal sight did not demand the respect and honor; it came because of the righteousness and truth which prevailed in his sight. There are times when men of high social structure may grace a room with their presence and all know they are there, only giving credit for such a short span of time. When Isaiah looked upon the Lord, the glory of the Lord and His train ***filled*** the temple. There is no comparison to the splendor and the magnificent beauty which only the Lord can provide, Isaiah realized this to be true.

The Seraphims

Standing above the throne were these beautiful servants of the Lord. This was a sight which left him speechless and very short of descriptive terms. These figures were similar to that of a man, only they had wings. Each had the face, feet and hands of man, and each spoke as a man would speak. The train of the Lord filled the Temple. This train was symbolical of the success or the victories the Lord has. When a king would parade through the streets in celebration of a victory, behind him would follow the spoils of victories he had won in order to show his prowess. Knowing that the Lord has never been and will never be defeated, the sight of His victories and battles won would have definitely been an awesome sight for humanity to see. One can only be reminded of the visitation on Mount Sinai by Moses, where he could only see the hinder part of the glory of the Lord; the majesty and beauty would have killed him.

Each creature had two wings which covered their feet and two wings which covered their face. With their faces covered, they could not look at the Lord, only bow in submission to His purity and glory. As every king has servants, some spend many years in training so they may be flawless and perform their duties with perfection. The prophet was aware of the servant's role and the importance of it to the king.

The seraphim seemed to have two duties: (1) to proclaim the holiness of the Lord and (2) to minister to men in search of holiness.[12] When Isaiah saw them, they were standing and crying one to another, proclaiming the holiness of the Lord. But when he cried out unto the Lord in verse five, the seraphim came and touched him with the coal from the altar; at this time they came to minister to him.

What Isaiah witnessed next was a shaking of the Temple. The Temple in the vision was doubtless that of Solomon's, one that Isaiah related to the sense of familiarity. The throne and the Temple are together as one in the vision. They were connected by His righteous train inside the Temple, and His all-encompassing glory outside which filled the whole earth. When the presence of the Lord moved into the Temple, it shook the very foundation.

This experience can be related to each person who desires a true and wholesome touch of the power of God. When we see the glory of the Lord in its fullness, it will most definitely shake us and the result will jar the foundation of our thinking. Everything that is ordinary and familiar to us will vanish when God becomes a part of our life. Worship moves, disturbs, and shakes our foundation in order that the Lord may move in.

When the seraphim touched his lips with the coal from the altar, the reality of his humanity showed its failure in the presence of Jehovah. It was then the cry from his lips changed to "woe is me!" and the sight and feeling overwhelmed him. Until we can see ourselves as God sees us, we can never be cleansed nor ministered unto. It is an attitude of our world of self-sufficient beings which get us into trouble. Until a man can look at himself, he will always be pointing out the faults of others around him.

A Personal Encounter

One of the most awesome encounters of this type happened a few years ago while in prayer, it is one which will live with me the rest of my life. As I was in an early morning meeting with the Lord, there seemed to be such a mighty presence of His power which filled the sanctuary where I had been praying. I have learned over the years to expect something every time I go to pray, but this particular morning what was about to transpire was beyond my greatest hopes and imaginations.

Many times in prayer, I have asked the Lord to search my heart and make sure there is nothing in it which would hinder His presence. Knowing I am human and live in a wicked world, I did not desire the spirits of the adversary to plant seeds of error which would destroy my spiritual walk and contact with Him. In a society where railing accusations are freely given, it is very easy to allow hatred, envy, and discord to reign. Every day we come in contact with those who are out to destroy us in order to make their "Christian" experience seem complete to themselves.

After a few hours of prayer, a powerful presence of the Lord swept in and seemed to fill the room as a mighty rain. While lying on the carpet, with my face toward the floor, I asked God (as I had done many times before) to search my heart and know it was right and pure. It seemed as if the spot light of heaven and the examination light began to sweep over me.

Suddenly, there seemed to be an out of the body experience taking place. As I lay there on the floor, I seemed to lift out of my body to a place much higher where I was looking down upon myself laying there. My body and soul seemed to take on a transparency which I had never thought of before. As I looked down upon myself, I could see straight through myself and even see the color of the carpet. I realized at this time exactly what the Lord saw when I came into His presence.

I was totally naked before His presence. Nothing could be hidden from the Almighty. There was never a chance that anything could be hidden, He sees and knows all. At this time, I realized exactly how Isaiah felt. The words of the book of Isaiah began to flow from my lips. The understanding of how God can actually see and examine me became ever so real.

Each day when I come into His presence, whether in prayer or just living, I now know how He sees me. It has made a difference to the way in which I live my life. We may fool others, but the God of eternity can see all that is within us. When people say things which are not true, when accusations are made, and the things which one may think are revealed; nothing matters as much as knowing that God knows and sees all. He who controls the eternal ages, made the world with the greatness of his voice and hands can know the deepest thoughts of the inner sanctum of the soul.

Reaching For Him

As we close these sections on the ministering spirits of the Lord, we have seen how great and effective they can be in our personal walk. But, just as in any great endeavor that is worthwhile – we need to maintain the proper avenue to accomplish it. For the next few moments, let us re-emphasize the important factors and steps which are vital to the accomplishment.

Prayer is the rail which moves the locomotive of our spirit toward God. If we do not have the time of personal communion with God, we can never know His will or desires. Our goals must be to please Him and Him alone. Just as we find John the Beloved, with his head leaning against the bosom of Jesus – we must also be close enough to God to hear his heartbeat. Notice the following passage, one which is referred to as the "song of desire for God" by the Psalmist David.

> Psalms 63:1-5 "O God, thou art my God; early will I seek thee: my soul thirsteth for thee, my flesh longeth for thee in a dry and thirsty land, where no water is;
>
> To see thy power and thy glory, so as I have seen thee in the sanctuary.
>
> Because thy lovingkindness is better than life, my lips shall praise thee.
>
> Thus will I bless thee while I live: I will lift up my hands in thy name.

> My soul shall be satisfied as with marrow and fatness; and my mouth shall praise thee with joyful lips:"

Prayer is the divine contact with God – it is the life source of all true existence. In order to survive this spiritual conflict, it is imperative that I spend time alone with the maker of my soul. Just as it is necessary for me to eat, drink and breathe in order to survive, the survival of my soul depends upon my contact and hearing the voice of God.

There are a lot of appointments which we consider important every day. We would never think of not going to the doctor when we are sick or not eating when we are hungry. Not one of us would decide it isn't necessary to go for a home closing – after all we would like to live in the house and own it; this is necessary in order to purchase the property. The value of our time with God is much, much more important than a home loan, food on the table or even the air which we breathe.

If there is anything I must do – I must pray!

If there is something which always must be done – I must pray!

If there are appointments I must keep – I must meet with God in prayer!

If there is someone I see often – I must frequently visit with God!

If there is an investment I must make – I must invest time in prayer![13]

It will be the desire of a child of God to spend time with Him. It is our desire to have our prayers heard by Him and to act favorably in His sight. God is no respecter of persons and loves each and every one of us; but God is a respecter of the heart. The heart which truly desires Him, that heart will he seek out. Our financial position in society, our age, gender or seniority within a company has no relationship to our walk with God.

God will not and has never been moved by our verbal usage and lengthy prayer. The flattery which gets men and women things they want in society or fine oratory ability will never work with the Almighty God. God looks upon the heart; nothing can be hidden from Him. We must remember that God knows our thoughts even before we ask or think. There are not any hidden magical formulas to getting in touch with this creator of the universe.

The only necessary ingredient which must be applied to our life is the honesty and integrity toward God. The only formula for success is prayer! Men and women who do not clean out their hearts do not hear from God. We must come before Him and realize we are an open book;

God only operates on one basic principle – the principles of His Word.

When the scriptures speak of praying continually, it does not mean we must pray every second, minute or hour of each day in order to have contact with God. But, we must have an attitude of prayer and listen to the voice of God as He leads us each day. There will be seasons of time where we will pray for lengthy sessions; these will give us the necessary food from the Throne of Heaven. Having a prayerful attitude is important, but we must seek the will and favor of God in all we do.

> Psalms 34:6-7 "This poor man cried, and the Lord heard him, and saved him out of all his troubles.
>
> The angel of the Lord encampeth round about them that fear him, and delivereth them."
>
> Psalms 34:17-18 "The righteous cry, and the Lord heareth, and delivereth them out of all their troubles.
>
> The Lord is nigh unto them that are of a broken heart; and saveth such as be of a contrite spirit."

There are times of peril when every man and woman will need to pray. We cannot wait for these times to come and start then. Someone once said there is no such thing as atheists in a fox hole under the fire of mortar shells. In the moments of danger when we have reached the end to our own resources, a man and woman will begin to pray.

Man's extremity is God's opportunity. But why should we live a life where we are made to pray, why not live a fulfilled life of joy and peace with a constant diet of time alone with God. The power that is available in pray is limitless because the maker of our soul is limitless. There is absolutely nothing which God cannot do, except sin. Through the avenue of prayer, as we have seen in the preceding chapters, God places His total resources within the reach of the believer. Remember the scripture in the book of Zechariah where the angel of the Lord told Joshua that "he would have full access to his courts." Prayer is the only hope and redemption we can have in this life.

How to Pray

Let us look at how we should pray, for as with every plan of action, there is a proper way. Just as God desires to give us access to the Courts of Heaven, there has to be a way which this approach must be made. Although it is impossible to visit this list in great detail, a quick overview will give us the starting place for successful use of the ministering spirits of God.

1. In His Name. In James 5:14, the Lord gave us the most assured way to receive from Him. There is no other power greater than the name of Jesus. This name will save from sin, heal the sick, and deliver all of mankind of any malady. It was in the name of Jesus that Peter prayed and the lame man at the gate Beautiful was healed.

2. Praying in faith. Prayer and faith go together, and one is dependent upon the other. Matthew 21:22 tells us "And all things, whatsoever ye shall ask in prayer, believing, ye shall receive." An unbeliever will not pray, but a man or woman who believes will pray and receive their needs from God. Faith does not believe that God can, but faith believes that God will. With faith we know the answer is assured. The common feelings of fear and doubt will leave with faith.

3. Effectual Prayer. Only the effectual prayer will get the desired results. Prayer is not the process of some type of liturgy or going through a series of words, prayer comes from the heart of man. It is the direct contact of the soul of man to the heartbeat of God. Effectual prayer will

allow the human spirit to reach out and receive that which comes directly from God.

4. Fervent Prayer. When prayer is recited, given as a series of obligations or read – they are not from the heart. A fervent prayer is one which can only come from deep within the bowels of a man or woman. A fervent prayer can only be prayed with a great sense of emotion, a fervor which is stirred inside the soul. An example of this comes from Hannah; her prayer was of such intensity that the priest thought she was drunk. Because of such fervent prayer, the child for which she longed was given to her by God.

5. Earnest Prayer. When we pray in earnest, we will see the hand of God move on our behalf. The scriptures are filled with men who prayed in this manner. Elijah was a man of human weakness, he was able to pray in earnest, and then a great rain came to the land in which he lived. Earnest prayer can only come from the deep seeded depths of desire and will consume us to the point where we will seek the wishes of God.

6. Keep Praying. When we continually bombard the kingdom of God with our prayers, a memorial is built up and God will hear and answer. We may have desires which we need God to give us an answer and a continual petition to Him will express the sincerity of our request. This example cannot be more profound than to look at the life of Cornelius, "a devout man, and one that feared God with all his house, which gave much alms to the people, and prayed to God alway." (Acts 10:2). Because of his continual praying, God saw his heart for salvation and sent Peter to his house; therefore, he was the first Gentile on which was poured out the Holy Ghost (Acts 10:44-48).[14]

Our Example in Prayer

There could be no greater example of the lifestyle which our communion with God should pattern after other than Jesus Christ. After being baptized in the Jordan River by John the Baptist, Jesus then went into the wilderness to pray and fast. As our example of how we are to overcome the flesh and sins of this world, His dedication to the importance of prayer gives us the victory.

The Apostles, Peter and John, are taught about often because of the miracles which were performed in their lives. One must take note of a number of situations which existed in their lives. At any given time, they were either going to the temple to pray or they had previously been in prayer.

Because of his trust in Jehovah; brought on by the time of prayer, Abraham had no doubt that God would provide a sacrifice when it was time to take the promise son Isaac to the mountain. His words were a declaration of the faith he had in Jehovah; "My son, God will provide himself a lamb for a burnt offering" (Genesis 22:8).

Let us not forget about Paul, a man who was struck down and blinded on the road to Damascus. After being converted he spent time alone in prayer and the result was deliverance from those who sought his life and being delivered from the chains in a prison cell because of prayer.

Conclusion

We can have all we desire from the King of Kings! If we will seek to find the complete will of God, nothing shall be lacking in our life. I trust that the reader will not think this another book, let it be an example of the power, confidence and trust which can be found in a walk with God.

What good does it do to know what I can have, only to live as a spiritual beggar? It is like a child who plays with a check book and writes check only to throw them away since there are no monetary funds available. The Kingdom of God is rich in blessings, hope, and life; let each reader seek after the things of God.

"Blessed is the man that endureth temptation: for when he is tried, he shall receive the crown of life, which the Lord hath promised to them that love him."

James 1:12

"But now is Christ risen from the dead, and become the firstfruits of them that slept.

For since by man came death, by man came also the resurrection of the dead.

For as in Adam all die, even so in Christ shall all be made alive.

But every man in his own order: Christ the firstfruits; afterward they that are Christ's at his coming."

I Corinthians 15:21-23

Fallen Angels

"Lest Satan should get an advantage of us: for we are not ignorant of his devices."

II Corinthians 2:11

Chapter Nine

Fallen Angels

Although it was not the original intentions of the author to include the fallen angels, a general knowledge and understanding will be helpful to the reader. It must be understood that all angels are not of God, some of them are the adversary to His purpose and bring confusion and hide the complete truth. The one thing that makes the "real" so valuable is the existence of the counterfeit.

Let us briefly examine these angels, what caused their state of affairs and how we may know and comprehend their work. These angels are in their condition of their on free will. Each one, although they do not have a soul that will die, will someday reap the eternal rewards of damnation.

> Jude 6 "And the angels which kept not their first estate, but left their own habitation, he hath reserved in everlasting chains under darkness unto the judgment of the great day."

We are clearly informed by the scriptures that a large number of angels who fell at one time had sinned. Although the scripture does not say in great detail concerning the nature of their transgression, we can only believe that their attitudes were that of their leader, Lucifer.

We do know that their basic work is to oppose God and do the work of Satan. Their goal is to afflict and deceive the people of God. By having knowledge of what is wrong and right, righteous and unrighteous; we can then make the choice on our own. Just as they made their own decision, we too must make the path which we choose.

Attitudes of Error

> Ezekiel 28:15-16 "Thou wast perfect in thy ways from the day that thou wast created, till iniquity was found in thee.
>
> By the multitude of thy merchandise they have filled the midst of thee with violence, and thou hast sinned: therefore I will cast thee as profane out of the mountain of God: and I will destroy thee, O covering cherub, from the midst of the stones of fire."

To every action which takes place, there are contributing factors. The same can be said of Satan and sin. How would the most beautiful angel in the Courts of Heaven trade all the splendor and beauty for eternal torment? What would cause a trusted confidant of the Almighty to stoop to such a low level and receive such horrendous rewards?

The Fall Begins

Take notice of the following scriptures from the writing of the book of Isaiah, this series of passages will give us an insight to why our world exist the way it does. The five steps, although very short, are very powerful avenues which lead all who choose them to destruction.

We can find that sin had its origin in heaven among the angelic creatures around the Throne of God. It is the rebellion in the heart of Lucifer that caused him to be cast down and the same attitude today which will lead to judgment for all humanity.

> Isaiah 14:12-16 "How art thou fallen from heaven, O Lucifer, son of the morning! how art thou cut down to the ground, which didst
> weaken the nations!

Is 14:13; For thou hast said in thine heart, I will ascend into heaven, I will exalt my throne above the stars of God: I will sit also upon the mount of the congregation, in the sides of the north:

Is 14:14; I will ascend above the heights of the clouds; I will be like the most High.

Is 14:15; Yet thou shalt be brought down to hell, to the sides of the pit.

Is 14:16; They that see thee shall narrowly look upon thee, and consider thee, saying, Is this the man that made the earth to tremble, that did shake kingdoms;"

As we review these attitudes, it is easy to see them in our modern society. By understanding and recognizing them, we can equip ourselves with the proper tools to be spiritually successful. Although these thoughts or spirits are common, it does not make them right.

1. I will ascend into the heavens. It is in this statement which reveals to us the exalted attitude which consumed Lucifer. Simply, it was his pride which hurled

him in the direction which he would be traveling. After all, he forgot who was his creator and the one in control of all things. Everything which he would do was only because of the higher authority that allowed it. When the pride began to grow in his heart, it blinded his vision and corrupted his wisdom. We must be careful not to become lifted up and think we are something. The blessings which we receive will either cause us to have humility, see our unworthiness or create vicious pride and we will become as fools.

2. I will exalt my throne above the stars of God. Pride creates selfishness and provokes egotism. The ultimate state of this condition causes one to make his or her own laws, own judge, own morality, and own god. This condition will cause one to go against God's will. From the state of rebellion flows contempt of the rights of others, excessive love of personal advancement, the desire to the spotlight, and intolerance of opinions that differ from our own. The more important the egotist feels himself to be, the more irritated he becomes when he

does not receive worship; those who flatter him are called wise; those who criticize him are condemned as fools.

3. <u>I will sit also upon the mount of the congregation</u>. It is here that a feeling of superiority, a "better than thou" attitude, seeking to destroy others for the sake of one's self. There is no room in this darkened abyss for anyone other than self. Self will do anything to promote self, and get to the top, regardless of the havoc caused by such exultation. We must be very careful in a world of large egos and personal ambitions; this attitude will reach the heart and has often reached into modern churches.

4. <u>I will ascend above the heights of the clouds</u>. Wisdom and honor can often corrupt. Where ever his home may have been, Satan's throne was just not high enough. He wanted to be a little higher. The attitude of "I" must be on top, the leader, or control the show will lead to the same position which Lucifer now has; as well as the same results. His heart had become corrupted, filled with the

glory of this position. We must be careful that we are not the ones who "must" control the show. There is an old saying that goes something like, "if it does not come from my chimney, it just ain't smoke." This attitude will destroy us both naturally and spiritually.

5. I will be like the most high. No longer was Lucifer satisfied with being one of the angels, but he was determined to take the place and authority away from God who gave him both the position and the beauty. All pride is void of mercy, love, goodness, kindness or any other benevolent factor. It is greedy, avaricious, envious, lustful, anger, gluttonous and all other distorted conditions of which can be thought. It manufactures its own gods, and directs is own paths and salutes its own praises, and sings its own songs. This spirit when loose within us can and will become a monster.[15]

Let us be careful of the fallen angels as well as the attitudes. This rebellion which was transferred to man in the Garden of Eden can completely control us. Satanic rebellion can only be conceived in our heart if we will allow it. Let each of us protect ourselves with prayer and time before the throne of God.

Scriptural References

There are a number of scriptural references to the qualities and judgments for the angels of Satan. Listed below are the scriptures and what the Bible calls them.

1. Fell with Lucifer from heaven (Isa. 14:12-14; Ezek. 28:11-17; Mt. 24:41; Rev. 12:7-12)
2. Hell is prepared for them (Mt. 24:41)
3. Oppose the saints (Rom. 8:38; Eph. 6:10-18)
4. Deceive men (II Cor. 11:14)
5. Subject to Christ (I Pet. 3:22)
6. Sinful and rebellious (Job 4:18; II Pet. 2:4; Jude 6,7; Rev. 12:7-9)
7. Evil (Ps. 78:49)
8. Will be punished (Mt. 24:41; Isa. 24:21-23; 25:7)
9. Cast out of heaven (Rev. 12:7-9)
10. Are organized (Eph. 1:21; 3:10; 6:10-17; Col. 2:10,15; Rev. 12:7-12)

Visitation of Angels

> ***"But while he thought on these things, behold, the angel of the LORD appeared unto him in a dream, saying, Joseph, thou son of David, fear not to take unto thee Mary thy wife: for that which is conceived in her is of the Holy Ghost."***
>
> ***Matthew 1:20***

Chapter Ten

Visitations of Angels

There were numerous occasions in the Bible where "mysterious" visitors were used to deliver a particular message. These visitors were spoken of as angels of the Lord. These references are for the reader to explore more in the scriptures.

Let each of us continue to remind ourselves of the blessings which we can have with a close walk with God. Those examples of scripture should give us the encouragement to know without a doubt that the Lord cares for each one.

1. The angel of the Lord told Hagar that she was pregnant with Abraham's son (Genesis 16:1-16, 21:17).

2. An angel of the Lord stopped Abraham just as he was about to sacrifice his son Isaac (Genesis 18:2, 22:1-19).

3. An angel of the Lord appeared to Moses in a burning bush and instructed him to lead the Israelites out of Egypt (Exodus 3:1-22).

4. An angel of the Lord stood poised to kill Balaam, whose life was spared because of the actions of his donkey (Numbers 22:21-38).

5. An angel of the Lord went to Bokim and told the Israelites he would not drive the pagan people out of the land of Canaan because they had made treaties with the people (Judges 2:1-7).

6. An angel of the Lord instructed Gideon to lead an Israelite attack against the mighty Midianites (Judges 6:11-40).

7. An angel of the Lord revealed to Manoah and his wife that they would have a son named Samson (Judges 13:1-25)

8. An angel of the Lord strengthened and encouraged Elijah (I Kings 19:1-9).

9. An angel of the Lord killed 185,000 Assyrian soldiers in one night (II Kings 19:35-36).

10. An angel of the Lord interpreted a series of visions for the prophet Zechariah (Zechariah 1:7-6:15).[16]

11. An angel of the Lord released the Apostles from prison (Acts 5:18-19).

12. An angel of the Lord was instrumental in bringing salvation to the house of Cornelius (Acts 10:3-7).

13. The angel Gabriel appeared to Mary to announce that she would have a child – Jesus (Luke 1:26-38).

14. While on a ship that was about to sink, Paul saw an angel with the message that he and the others would be spared (Acts 27:23-26).

15. Peter was set free from prison by an angel of the Lord (Acts 12:4-10).

16. An angel of the Lord rolled back the stone from the tomb where Jesus lay (Matthew 28:2-7).

Visitations from Genesis

In the book of Genesis, chapter 19; there were eight commands given by the angel of the Lord to Lot and his wife. After much prayer by his uncle, Abraham to spare him and possibly the city of Sodom and Gomorrah – the angels came to direct Lot from the fire and brimstone which would be poured out upon the city where he lived.

Since there were not enough righteous in the city for God to save it, the Lord answered the prayer of Abraham and sent the angels to save his nephew for the horrible wrath which was to come. Listed below are the directives from the angel:

1. Arise (vs. 15)
2. Take your wife and daughters (vs. 17)
3. Escape for your life (vs. 17)
4. Look not behind you (vs. 17)
5. Do not stay in the plain (vs. 17)
6. Escape to the mountain (vs. 17)
7. Make haste (vs. 22)
8. Escape (vs. 22)

Visitation from Judges:

In the book of Judges, chapter thirteen; the children of Israel were in the hands of the Philistines. A family in the tribe of Dan, whose name was Manoah; had a wife which was barren and bare not; a curse which no family wanted. After much prayer for a child, the angel of the Lord visited them and delivered the answer to their prayers.

1. You shall conceive and bare a son (vs. 3)
2. He shall begin to deliver Israel from the hand of the Philistines (vs.5)
3. He shall be a Nazarite from his mother's womb (vs. 5)

Commands given to Manoah and his wife:

1. (Wife) Beware, and drink no wine or strong drink (vs. 4, 7, 14)
2. Eat no unclean thing (vs. 7)
3. No razor shall come upon his (your son) head (vs. 5)
4. Do not eat anything that comes from the vine (vs. 14)
5. (Manoah) All that I have commanded her, let her obey (vs. 13)

In Judges, chapter six; the children of Israel were captive to the Medianites for seven years. The children of Israel began to pray for Jehovah to send them a deliverer. They had become greatly impoverished and their living conditions worsened – their cry to the Lord was finally heard.

The Lord sent a prophet to Israel (vs. 8) and sent an angel to give him the directions which he needed.

1. The angel came from the Lord (vs. 11)
2. Sat under an oak tree (vs. 11)
3. Appeared to Gideon (vs. 12)
4. Said, "The Lord is with thee" (vs. 12)
5. Looked upon him (vs. 14)
6. Said, "Go in this thy might" (vs. 14)
7. Sent Gideon to deliver Israel (vs. 14)
8. Prophesied to Gideon (vs. 16)
9. Made a promise, "I will tarry.." (vs. 18)
10. Commanded Gideon (vs. 20)
11. Put forth the end of the staff that was in His hand, and touched the meal Gideon had prepared for Him (vs. 21)
12. Departed out of his sight (vs. 21)

Ministry in the Book of Acts

1. Deliverance of the Apostle from jail (5:19)
2. Directing Philip where to preach (8:26)
3. Directing Cornelius where to find a preacher so he could be saved (10:3, 7 22)
4. Deliverance to Peter from jail (12:7-11, 15)
5. Destruction of Herod for pride (12:23)
6. Directing and comforting Paul (27:23)

Angelic Appearances to Men

1. Hager (2 times – Gen. 16:7-11; 21:17)
2. Abraham (3 times – Gen. 18:2; 22:11, 15)
3. Lot and Sodomites (Gen. 19:1-22)
4. Jacob (2 times – Gen. 28:12, 31:11; 32:1)
5. Moses (Ex. 3:2)
6. Balaam (Num. 22:22-35)
7. Joshua (5:15; Ex. 23:20-23; 32:34)
8. Israel (Judg. 2:1-5)
9. Gideon (Judg. 6:11-22)
10. Manoah's wife (Judg. 13:3-5)
11. Manoah and wife (Judg. 13:9-21)
12. David (2 Sam. 24:1; I Chr 21)
13. Elijah (4 times – I Ki. 19:5-7; II Ki. 1:3, 15)
14. Elisha and servant (II Ki. 6:16-17)
15. Assyrians (II Ki. 19:35; Isa. 37:36)
16. Hebrew Children (Dan. 3:25-28)

17. Nebuchadnezzar (Dan. 3:24-25)
18. Daniel (5 times – Dan. 6:22; 8:16; 9:21; 10:5-21; 12:5-7)
19. Zechariah (7 times – Zech. 1:8-19; 2:3; 3:1-6; 4:1-5; 5:5-10; 6:4-5; 12:8)
20. Joseph (3 times – Mt. 1:20; 2:13,19)
21. Mary (Lk. 1:26-38)
22. Zacharias (Lk. 1: 5-20)
23. Shepherds (Lk. 2:9-14)
24. Jesus (2 times – Mt. 4:11; Lk. 22:43)
25. Women (Mt. 28: 1-5)
26. Disciples (Acts 1:11)
27. Peter and John (Acts 5:19)
28. Philip (Acts 8:26)
29. Cornelius (Acts 10:3, 30-32)
30. Peter (Acts 12:7-11)
31. Paul (Acts 27:23)
32. John (52 times in the book of Revelation)

And he dreamed, and behold a ladder set up on the earth, and the top of it reached to heaven: and behold the angels of God ascending and descending on it.

Genesis 28:12

New Age Philosophy

> ***"Lest Satan should get an advantage of us: for we are not ignorant of his devices."***
>
> ***II Corinthians 2:11***

Chapter Eleven

New Age Philosophy

New Age is the term commonly used to designate the broad movement of late 20th century and contemporary Western culture, characterized by an eclectic and individual approach to spiritual exploration. Self-spirituality, New-spirituality, and Mind-body-spirit are other names sometimes used for the movement. The New Age is a diverse movement of individuals including many who graft new age beliefs onto a traditional religious affiliation. Recent surveys of U.S. adults indicate that around 20% of Americans hold at least some New Age beliefs

Definition of New Age

Though there are no formal or definitive boundaries for membership, those who are likely to sample many diverse teachings and practices (from both 'mainstream' and 'fringe' traditions) and to formulate their own beliefs and practices based on their experiences can be considered as New Age Rather than following the lead of an organized religion, "New Agers" typically construct their own spiritual journey based on material taken as needed from the mystical traditions of the world's religions, also including shamanism, neo-paganism and occultism.

New Age practices and beliefs may be characterized as a form of alternative spirituality or alternative religion. Even apparent exceptions, such as alternative medicine or traditional medicine practices, often have some spiritual dimension — such as a conceptual integration of mind, body, and spirit.

The term New Age is used in a Western or modern context where the Judeo-Christian tradition and/or Positivism are dominant, so the use of "alternative" in New Age thought generally implies a contrast with these dominant religious and/or scientific beliefs. Hence, many New Age ideas and practices in the West contain either explicit or implied critiques of organized mainstream Christianity—emphasis on meditation suggests that simple prayer and faith is insufficient, and beliefs such as reincarnation (which not all New Age followers accept) challenge familiar Christian doctrines, like those regarding the Afterlife.

History

The contemporary usage of the term New Age was popularized by the American mass media during the late 1980s, to describe the alternative spiritual subculture focused on meditation, channeling, reincarnation, crystals, psychic experience, holistic health, environmentalism, other fields associated with pseudoscience and anomalous phenomena, and various "unsolved mysteries" such as UFOs, Earth mysteries and crop circles. Typical activities of this subculture include participation in study or meditation groups, attendance at lectures and fairs; the purchase of books, music, and other products such as crystals or incense; and patronage of fortune-tellers, healers and spiritual counselors

The New Age subculture already existed in the 1970's, and continued themes from the 1960's counterculture Earlier generations would have recognized some, but not all, of the New Age's constituent elements under the practices of Spiritualism, Theosophy, or some forms of New Thought orf the Metaphysical movement, all of which date back to the nineteenth century, as does alternative health. These movements in turn have roots in Transcendentalism, Mesmerism, Swedenborgianism, and various earlier Western esoteric or occult traditions, such as the Hermetic arts of astrology, magic, alchemy, and cabbala.

In the English-speaking world, we should make special mention of study groups devoted to American trance-diagnostician Edgar Cayce, who inspired many of today's channelers. The British neo-Theosophist Alice Bailey's writings may have supplied the term New Age (or New Era) in reference to the transition from the astrological age of Pisces to that of Aquarius. Another claimant for the term is the American artist mystic and philosopher Walter Russell spoke in an essay of "...this New Age philosophy of the spiritual re-awakening of man..." published in 1944. The Findhorn Foundation, an early New Age intentional community in northern Scotland founded in 1962 played a significant role. The movement in Russia has been heavily influenced by the legacy of Nicholas Roerich and Helena Roerich, who taught in the Theosophical tradition. Another former Theosophist, Rudolf Steiner and his anthroposophical movement, is a major influence, especially upon German-speaking New Agers. In Brazil, followers of Spiritist writer Allan Kardec blend with the Africanized folk traditions of Candomblé and Umbanda.

Key moments in raising public awareness of this subculture include the publication of Linda Goodman's best selling astrology books Sun Signs (1968) and Love Signs (1978), the Harmonic Convergence organized by Jose Arguelles in Sedona, Arizona in 1987; and the wave of interest in the broadcast of Shirley MacLaine's television mini-series Out on a Limb (also 1987). This was an autobiographical account of her mid-life spiritual exploration. Also influential are the claims of channelers such as Jane Roberts (Seth) and J.Z. Knight (Ramtha), as well as revealed writings such as A Course In Miracles (Helen Schucman), The Celestine Prophecy (James Redfield), Mutant Message Down Under (Marlo Morgan), Conversations with God (Neale Donald Walsch), and Love Without End: Jesus Speaks by Glenda Green.

The question of which contemporary cultural elements ought to be included under the name of "New Age" is quite vexing. New Age channelers have many points of similarity with Spiritualist mediums. Many spiritual movements, such as neo-paganism and transpersonal psychology partially overlap with it. Many groups prefer to distance themselves from the possible negative connotations of the "New Age" name such as the media hoopla, commercialism, and perhaps hucksterism. For example, key individuals in the New Thought Movement, such as Ernest Holmes, have focused on a more scientific approach and do not share New Age beliefs in reincarnation, magic, or channeling.

Major attempts to present the New Age as a values-based sociopolitical movement included Mark Satin's New Age Politics (orig. 1976), Theodore Roszak's Person/Planet (1978), Marilyn Ferguson's Aquarian Conspiracy (1980), and Gordon Davidson and Corinne McLaughlin's Spiritual Politics (1994). The New Age is a wide menu of ideas and activities, from which participants in the subculture select their own preferred streams to patronize or identify with.

Since around 2000 the New Age movement is sometimes referred to as the New Edge movement when it is closely allied to ecological and environmental concerns.

Belief of the New Age

Those who categorize themselves as New Age followers have multifarious beliefs; nevertheless, certain themes emerge. An individual who identifies with the New Age may subscribe to some or all of these, depending on their own sense of what is right and wrong.

All humanity—indeed all life, everything in the universe—is spiritually interconnected, participating in the same energy. "God" is one name for this energy.

Spiritual beings (e.g. angels, ascended masters, elementals, ghosts, and/or space aliens) exist, and will guide us, if we open ourselves to their guidance.

The human mind has deep levels and vast powers, which are capable even of overriding physical reality. "You create your own reality." Nevertheless, this is subject to certain spiritual laws, such as the principle of cause and effect (karma).

Children are being born today with a more highly developed spiritual power than earlier generations.

The individual has a purpose here on earth, in the present surroundings, because there is a lesson to learn. The most important lesson is love.

Death is not the end; there is only life in different forms. What some refer to as an afterlife does not punish us but teaches us, perhaps through the mechanisms of reincarnation or near-death experiences.

Intuition or "divine guidance" is a more appropriate guide than rationalism, scientific skepticism, or the scientific method.

Western science wrongly neglects such things as parapsychology, meditation, and holistic health.

There exists a mystical core within all religions, Eastern and Western. Dogma and religious identity are not so important. The Bible is considered by some, but not all, to be a wise and holy book. Many important truths are found in the Bible, or are referred to only very obliquely. Some say that Jesus was an Essene, or that he traveled to India in his youth to study Eastern religions. Others say that Jesus was a later avatar of the Buddha.

Feminine forms of spirituality, including feminine images of the divine, such as the female Aeon Sophia in Gnosticism, have been subordinated, masked, or obliterated by patriarchal movements that were widely practiced when sacred teachings were first committed to writing. A renaissance of the feminine is particularly appropriate at this time.

Meditation, yoga, t'ai chi ch'üan, reiki, and other Eastern practices are valuable and worthwhile.

A certain critical mass of people with a highly spiritual consciousness will bring about a sudden change in the whole population.

Science and spirituality are ultimately harmonious. New discoveries in science, e.g. evolution and quantum mechanics, when rightly understood, point to spiritual principles.

An appeal to the language of nature and mathematics, as evidenced by numerology in Kabbala, gnosticism etc., to discern the nature of god.

We have a responsibility to take part in positive creative activity and to work to heal ourselves, each other and the planet.

The food you eat has an effect on your mind as well as your body. It is generally preferable to eat fresh organic vegetarian food which is locally grown and in season. Raw food and sprouted seeds have a particularly spirit enhancing quality.

Fasting can help you achieve higher levels of consciousness.

Ultimately every interpersonal relationship has the potential to be a helpful experience in terms of our own growth. We learn about ourselves through our relationships with other people by getting to see what we need to work on ourselves and what strengths we bring to the other party in order to help them in their life. All our relationships are destined to be repeated until they are healed, if necessary over many lifetimes. As Souls seeking wholeness, our goal is eventually to learn to love everyone we come in contact with.

Ancient civilizations such as Atlantis may truly have existed, leaving behind certain relics and monuments (the Great Pyramid, Stonehenge) whose true nature has not been discovered by mainstream historians.

Certain geographic locations emanate special energy, which may be male or female in character. Many such places may have been considered sacred in the world religions or as healing places by indigenous native populations.

Rocks and crystals have special psychic energies and can be an aid to meditation and healing.

There are no coincidences. Everything around you has spiritual meaning, and spiritual lessons to teach you. You are meant to be here, and are always exactly where you need to be to learn from what confronts you.

The mind has hidden powers and abilities, which have a spiritual significance.

Dreams and psychic experiences are ways in which our souls express themselves.

A positive attitude supported by affirmations will achieve success in anything.

There is a cosmic goal. There is typically a belief that all entities are (willingly or unwillingly) cooperating in some cosmic goal of achieving a "higher" or more complete coherence with a cosmic "consciousness" (or some other goal state of "goodness"), often described as an evolutionary process or simply to learn. This underlying cosmic goal gives direction to all events, reducing the concept of coincidence to one of ignorance of hidden meaning.

This is a time of great transformation for the Earth and human consciousness. Certain dates have a special significance in these changes. 1986 and the Harmonic Convergence was one, and there are others to come in 2011 or 2012.

(Note: The above information is from Wikipedia, the free encyclopedia. Version 1.2, November 2002) Copyright © 2000,2001,2002 Free Software Foundation, Inc. 51 Franklin St., Fifth Floor, Boston, MA 02110-1301 USA.

Biblical Responses to the New Age Movement

1. God is personal. If God were impersonal, then the following qualities could not be His.

   a. God speaks and has a self given name: "I AM" (Exodus 3:14).

   b. God is long suffering, (Psalm 86:15; 2 Peter 3:15).

   c. God is forgiving (Daniel 9:9; Ephesians 1:7; Psalm 86:5).

   d. God hates sin (Psalm 5:5-6; Habakkuk 1:13).

2. Man is not divine, but a sinner (Romans 3:23).

   a. He is deceitful and desperately wicked (Jer. 17:9).

b. He is full of evil (Mark 7:21-23).

c. He loves darkness rather than light (John 3:19).

d. He is unrighteous, does not understand and does not seek for God (Rom. 3:10-12).

e. He is helpless and ungodly (Rom. 5:6).

f. He is dead in his trespasses and sins (Eph. 2:1).

g. He is by nature a child of wrath (Eph. 2:3).

h. He cannot understand spiritual things (1 Cor. 2:14).

3. Salvation is not correct thoughts, but deliverance from the consequence of our sin (Romans 6:23; Ephesians 2:8-9).

    a. Salvation is God's deliverance from damnation (Eph. 2:8-9; Rom. 1:18; 2:5; 5:9).

    b. This salvation is found in no one but Jesus alone (Acts 4:12).

4. Miracles are from God not from the mind of man (Matthew 8:1-4; Mark 6:30-44; Luke 17:12-19; John 2:1-11).

    a. Miracles imply an action by someone that is greater than the individual. If God is impersonal, miracles cannot occur. But they do occur today as well as in Bible times and are not simply proper thoughts or understanding.

5. Christ means "anointed. Jesus was the Christ, the anointed one." It does not mean a consciousness or quality of people. Jesus was Christ, Messiah and the Deliverer from sin.

    a. Jesus is the Christ (Matt. 16:16,20; Luke 9:20).

    b. "Was it not necessary for the Christ to suffer these things and to enter into His glory" (Luke 24:26).

    c. "Thus it is written, that the Christ should suffer and rise again from the dead the third day" (Luke 24:46).

    d. "...we have found the Messiah (which translated means Christ)" (John 1:41).

e. "He [David] looked ahead and spoke of the resurrection of the Christ..." (Acts 2:31).

f. "...God has made Him both Lord and Christ this Jesus whom you crucified" (Acts 2:36).

g. "For while we were still helpless, at the right time Christ died for the ungodly" (Rom. 5:6).

h. "Therefore we have been buried with Him through baptism into death, in order that as Christ was raised from the dead through the glory of the Father, so we too might walk in newness of life" (Rom. 6:4).

i. Christ is crucified (1 Cor. 1:23).

j. Humanity will sin against Christ (1 Cor. 8:12).

k. The blood of Christ (1 Cor. 10:16).

6. Only the Bible has the message of Grace. Grace is the unmerited favor of God upon His people. Grace is the undeserved kindness of God. Grace is getting the blessings we do not deserve. At the death of Christ we are blessed; we are given grace; we are given eternal life and forgiveness of sins. Only Christianity has the message of free forgiveness given.

7. Humanity is not unlimited, but just the opposite: it is under bondage (Romans 5:12). Sin is its master and a deadly and deceitful one at that.

8. True morality is that which is revealed by God in the Bible (Exodus 20). Anything else is only an imitation, a set of ideas laid down by man that originate from the mind of sinful man.

9. The Bible opposes almost all the tenets of the New Age Movement. As Christians, we should be watchful to recognize what is false and teach what is true. We should be wary because the Edenic lie still rings strong in the hearts of the deceived -- and they want us to believe as they.

Closing Thought

In April of 2008, I was offered a job near New Orleans, Louisiana. The job offer was pretty good but I was not prepared for what "benefits" would exist when we arrived. We would live in a home which was over seventy-five years old and had been occupied by many different people, some with little or no moral character.

After about eight months at the residency, Karen became very disturbed by what she had seen and the effect it was having on our relationship. Since we had been married, there had never been a disagreement or argument between the two of us and suddenly we could not agree on anything. For some unknown reason, everything became an issue which was very difficult to resolve.

Late one evening when I came home from work, my wife spoke to me of something which she had been seeing for the past few months. As she would stand in the kitchen or work at her desk in an extra room, a "dark figure" would seem to haunt her at every turn. It was like the spirit was trying to constantly remind her of its presence and was not going anywhere.

A few days later, once again we began to anoint every door, window and room. It was at the anointing of the rooms that we spoke to the adversary, "In the Name of Jesus, we command you to leave this home and return to where you came from." Methodically going from room to room and at each location (doors and windows), we completely saturated our home with the "blood of Jesus."

Since this anointing, we have never had any problems. It is the firm belief of this author and his wife, if we will use the power available from the scriptures – a great peace and happiness can be found in our homes.

Tsavah: Appointing the Anointing

Born-again believers can actually appoint the power of God! Much like the secretary who makes appointments for the lawyer, we can make appointments for God. How?

Notice Isaiah 45:11,12; "Thus saith the Lord, the Holy One of Israel, and his Maker, Ask me of things to come concerning my sons, and concerning the work of my hands command ye me.I have made the earth, and created man upon it: I, even my hands, have stretched out the heavens, and all their host have I commanded."

God told Isaiah, "Command ye me!" Can we command God? No! Not in the sense of ordering God around at our will. Moreover, it is altogether possible to command God at His will.

God only answers prayer if it is according to His will. (If we seek his will, then we will learn to pray according to that will and purpose.)

The Hebrew word command is *tsavah* which means to appoint. In this case it means to appoint to a specific task. God told Isaiah, "Concerning my sons, and ... the work of my hands, command ye me." He actually asked Isaiah to appoint Him to work in the lives of the inhabitants of the earth. There are certain things that God desires to do, but we must appoint Him. We must appoint God to our lost loved ones. We must appoint Him to those who are sick and dying. We must appoint God to our cities, nations, and the world.

As believers we must strive to fulfill God's original purpose for mankind. We must repair the breach! Our prayer lives must contain everything God has available. If not, we are not fully accessing God's purpose for prayer.

Isaiah foresaw a group of people who would repair and restore the ruins caused by the first breach. He said,

"And they that shall he of thee shall build up the old waste places: thou shalt raise up the foundations of many generations; and thou shalt be called the Repairer of the Breach. The restorer of the paths to dwell in." (Isaiah 58:12). Notice, Isaiah plainly said, "the Repairer of the Breach."

The word *breach* here is singular while the words places, foundations, and paths are all plural; meaning that all the destruction of the places, foundations, and paths is due to the *one breach*. Every breach, gap, or hedge we must pray for today is a direct product of Eden's breach. **How do we repair this breach? How do we reconnect the natural to the supernatural? How do we step beyond the wiles of the enemy and access God's original intentions for mankind?**

We transcend beyond Satan's present authority when fellowship with God is restored. Micah 4:8 speaks of the first dominion or lease being restored. "And thou, O tower of the flock, the strong hold of the daughter of Zion, unto thee shall it come, even the first dominion; the kingdom shall come to the daughter of Jerusalem."

The Matthew Henry Commentary tells us that this scripture refers to the Church. Ellen G. White, a prominent spiritual author, also explains how the first dominion refers to Adam's original lease and authority. She says, "All that was lost by the first Adam will be restored by the second Adam."

How do we receive this restoration? Under the new covenant, fellowship is restored through faith in Christ's work at Calvary. Spiritual death is the chasm of lost fellowship. This being true, restored fellowship gives us the authority that the first leaseholder had. Here is the proof.

"For whosoever is born of God overcometh the world (kosmos); and this is the victory that overcometh the world (kosmos), even our faith." (I John 5:4)

"Ye are of God .. , and have overcome them: because greater is He that is in you than he that is in the world (kosmos)". (I John 4:4)

Prayer connects the natural world to the supernatural world. Again, the breach which must be repaired is the separation of these realms. When Christ came as the intercessor for the transgressors, the fissure between the natural and the supernatural was welded shut. Now, through Christ, we can have full access to the supernatural. We as believers have the same ability to restore the supernatural. Through Christ we are free from Eden's breach and Satan's power. We are the repairers of the breach!

Endnotes

1. Nelson's Illustrated Bible Dictionary, 1986, Thomas Nelson Publishers
2. James Moffatt Translation, Harper & Row, Publishers, p.1027
3. The Zondervan Pictoral Bible Dictionary, 1963, Zondervan Publishing
4. Ibid.
5. Ibid
6. Ibid
7. Ibid
8. Nelson's Illustrated Bible Dictionary, 1986, Thomas Nelson Publishers
9. Unger's Bible Dictionary, Moody Press, p. 191
10. Ibid
11. The Way of Victorious Praying, Zacharias Tanee Fomum, Vantage Press
12. The Call To Worship, Pentecostal Publishing House, p. 81
13. Fundamental Bible Lessons II, C. L. Dees, p. 8
14. The Mysteries and Intrigues of the Bible, Tyndale House Publishers, Inc., p. 146

Syd D., CEO and Missionary for NationsLight Ministeries (North Carolina)

"This is fantastic stuff here. Wish I had a way of getting it into all the earth."

Linda and Donald D., Texas

"I can say it has blessed Donald and me more than you will ever know. It has taught us to understand the Spirit of God around us. God has sent this to us. We have really been moved and renewed by the Spirit of God."

Robert E. Louisiana

"After reading this book, I have been made to realize that we live far beneath our benefits that God has provided us by the Angels. This book is awesome, and you will not want to stop reading it. The author must have had a personal experience with the Angels; you can feel it as you read this book."

Andrew K., North Carolina

"Understanding the Angels is truly a "must read" book on a subject little has been written and understood. The author's immersion of his personal experiences is quite moving and compelling."

For additional information regarding book orders, interviews and speaking engagements, please send your request to: jameshodges@lightandlamp.com